Basel Mission Education
in Cameroon

Series information:
SPEARS STUDIES IN AFRICAN AND AFRICAN DIASPORA HISTORY

Series Editor
Womai I. Song
Earlham College, Indiana

Editorial Reading Panel
George Njung (Wits University)
Bridget Teboh (UMass Dartmouth)
Francis Dube (Morgan State University)
Walters Nkwi (Leiden University & University of Buea)
George Kintiba (University of Maryland, College Park)

Series Description
The series is interested in a variety of titles that range from single monographs to edited volumes insofar as they engage with issues of African history and the diaspora. Area specializations that may be considered by the board include but are not limited to economic, political and social history. The board is especially interested in accounts of people's economic and social activities during the colonial and postcolonial periods – e.g. fashion, dress, labour unions, education, youth, religion and religious movements, journalism, popular culture, literature, film, art, and women's histories.

To submit a proposal for the book series, include the following core items: a) a concise description of the book, outlining your rationale, approach, main themes, objectives and any unique features; b) an abstract of about 200-300 words; c) a table of contents and d) a sample chapter, preferably, the introduction. Should you prefer to be more detailed, a proposal form is available for completion. Send your complete proposal to the series editor at songwo@earlham.edu

Basel Mission Education in Cameroon

1886-1968

Mathew B. Gwanfogbe

Spears Books
Denver, Colorado

Spears Books
An Imprint of Spears Media Press LLC
7830 W. Alameda Ave, Suite 103-247
Denver, CO 80226
United States of America

First Published in the United States of America in 2020 by Spears Books
www.spearsmedia.com
info@spearsmedia.com
Information on this title: www.spearsmedia.com/basel-mission-education-in-cameroon

© 2020 Mathew B. Gwanfogbe
All rights reserved.

No part of this publication may be reproduced, distributed, or transmitted in any form or by any means, including photocopying, recording, or other electronic or mechanical methods, without the prior written permission of the publisher, except in the case of brief quotations embodied in critical reviews and certain other noncommercial uses permitted by copyright law. For permission requests, write to the publisher, addressed "Attention: Permissions Coordinator," at the above address.

ISBN: 9781942876687 (Paperback)
ISBN: 9781942876694 (eBook)

Spears Media Press has no responsibility for the persistence or accuracy of urls for external or third-party internet websites referred to in this publication, and does not guarantee that any content on such websites is, or will remain, accurate or appropriate.

Designed and typeset by Spears Media Press LLC
Cover designed by Doh Kambem

Distributed globally by African Books Collective (ABC)
www.africanbookscollective.com

To the memory of All BM/PCC Teachers and Educators

Contents

Figures   x
Tables   xi
Foreword   xiii
Acknowledgements   xv
Abbreviations   xvi

INTRODUCTION   1
   Post-WW1 Missionary Resumption   2

CHAPTER ONE   9
   Basel Mission Education Under German Colonial Administration   9
      BM Background and Choice   10
      BM and Colonial Collaboration   11
      BM and the British Baptist Missionary Society   14

CHAPTER TWO   17
   Setting up Basel Mission Education in Cameroon   17
      Problems of Expansion   18
      BM Educational Objectives   19
      Organization of BM Schools   20
      Four School Types   21
      BM Education Problems and Reform Attempts   26
      Rival Missionary Societies   28
      Internal Hurdles of BM Education Reforms   32
      Bohner and the BM Education Goal   32
      Training Centres   37

CHAPTER THREE — 43
Basel Mission Education and The German Regime — 43
Exploitation — 44
BM Education and Other Missionary Societies — 48
BM Educational Achievements under the German Administration — 49

CHAPTER FOUR — 53
Cameroonian Responses to Basel Mission Education under the German Regime — 53

CHAPTER FIVE — 63
Basel Mission Education under British and Postcolonial Regimes: 1916-1966 — 63
WWI and the Non-Missionary Period – 1914-1925 — 64
The Mandate — 68
After World War I — 69
Trusteeship to Postcolonial Period — 79
Teacher Training — 81
Female Education — 84
Secondary Education — 87
Vocational/Technical Education — 91
The Handing-Over — 92

CHAPTER SIX — 97
Cameroonian Reactions to Basel Mission Education During the British Regimes — 97

CHAPTER SEVEN — 107
Basel Mission Education to PCC — 107
Stage One — 107
Stage Two — 107
Stage Three — 108
Preparation of Cameroonian Church Leaders — 108
Handing-over of Schools — 112

CONCLUSION **115**
    Afterword 117
    Appendix 119
    References 123
    Index 131

ILLUSTRATIONS

FIGURES

FIGURE 1.1. Julius von Soden, First German Governor of Cameroon (1885-1891)   13

FIGURE 2.1. Basel Mission School, Buea   23

FIGURE 2.2. Rev. Schuler, Knighted by Fon Fonyonga II at the Palace Court   35

FIGURE 4.1. Basel Mission House Bali   55

FIGURE 4.2. BM School Bali (first school in the Grassfields): staff, pupils and the Fon at the front rank 1905   56

FIGURE 4.3. Governor Jesco Von Puttkamer (1895 – 1906) 58

FIGURE 5.1. Basel Mission School Besongabang   74

FIGURE 5.2. Fritz Raaflaub, veteran inter-war-years educator   77

FIGURE 5.3. Basel Mission Teachers Training College Batibo   82

FIGURE 5.4. Basel Mission Teachers Training College Nyasoso (founded in 1963)   82

FIGURE 5.5. Hon Solomon Tandeng Muna   83

FIGURE 5.6. (Lina Weber) Na Weber, driving force of BM female education Mission   85

FIGURE 5.7. D. H. O'Neil, Pioneer Principal, BM College   88

FIGURE 5.8. J.A. Ozimba, pioneer Senior African Tutor, Basel Mission College, Bali (1949-1957)   88

FIGURE 5.9. Current main block of CPC Bali   89

FIGURE 5.10. Dr. & Mrs Peter Rudin-Principal, (extreme left and right) with Mr & Mrs Donald Whitt – Vice Principal (middle)   89

FIGURE 7.1. The Rev. Peter Esoka, first Synod Chairman (Moderator)   110
FIGURE 7.2. Jacob Shu, first Synod vice-chairman   111
FIGURE 7.3. Eugene Ekiti, pioneer Cameroonian Education Secretary   111
FIGURE 7.4. Rt. Rev. Abraham Ebong Ngole (1899-1980), First PCC Moderator   112

TABLES
Table 3.1. The Evolution of School Enrolment during German Annexation   49
Table 3.2. Schools and enrolments by 1912   51
Table 5.1. BM Schools Enrolments during the Mandate Period   75
Table 5.2. Decline of Vernacular Schools Enrolments during the Postwar Era   80
Table 5.3. BM Schools Enrolment in the Decolonization Period (1945-1966)   81
Table 6.1. 1943 Elementary Schools Results per Agency   104
Table 7.1. BM Educational Establishments Handed over to PCC   113
Presbyterian Education Authority (PEA) Education Secretaries from 1968 to Date   119

FOREWORD

Professor Mathew B. Gwanfogbe has painstakingly documented the convoluted beginnings of the history of Western education in Cameroon. And since it is said that a people without knowledge of its history perishes, his storehouse of the relevant pieces of history that form the foundations of that educational history is carefully selected and explored. Cameroon and its current educational agenda must be faulted for ignorance of this past. For a lot of challenges devolve on that ignorance. This is an essential work, and one wonders why it was not indexed until now and how Cameroon's educational history can ever have been discussed with any seriousness without this perspicacious document.

I believe that noting the processes of education as inextricably tied to the history of the Basel Mission in Cameroon will light up the meaning and purpose of present educational pursuits and problems. The solutions to the challenges are also embedded in the trial and error realizations of those days. It is for this reason that I strongly hold that this work provides a guided future to the educational and political programmes of Cameroon. By this I do not in any way intend to underrate the depths of the analysis and the refined piecing together of informational nuggets to form this organic whole that so titillates the mind. For the end picture is one of interlaced jagged edges of political, religious, private and public motives all carefully laid at the feet of Basel Mission endeavours. This study in this light constitutes sheer intellectual delight.

For the Basel Mission, it is a proud past to look at, particularly when that past vindicates the Missions against side accusations of racist and exploitative collusions with colonial regimes against the Africans. True, it is not an altogether rosy past, considering the errors that were committed. Yet, it is flattering to note that most of the errors were process errors rather than systemic ones and that in policy and general perception, the missions stood firm for the faith with education as a means for its spread. It is equally heart-warming to find documentation that stands out as tribute to those who bore the brunt of the difficulties or who did their best to resolve the great challenges that surfaced. These daring and diligent individuals would otherwise be forgotten. For, when merits and total efforts fail to be acknowledged, it is truly frustrating. The likes of missionaries and Cameroonians who sacrificed their lives must smile from their eternal abode at this remembrance of them placed in the integral folds of genuine historical research. But it is not for the dead alone to smile: all who now constitute relay points for the batons of educational and developmental continuity, noting this acknowledgement, should celebrate their own status as pieces of the great continuum. This then is a valid document for use in curriculum development, political lessons and evangelical processes, on the one hand, and on training in people management, cultural integration/inculturation of Africanity in the churches as well as the strategic integration of secular governance in evangelical needs. Read between the lines, this is a work with very wide-ranging appeals and interests. I can only appeal that it be given the widest publicity for greater readership, influence and overall impact.

Rt. Rev. Samuel F. Fonki (PCC Moderator)

ACKNOWLEDGEMENTS

I owe huge debts of gratitude to my former students and colleagues who read and corrected or made suggestions for this book. Professors Richard Aldrich, Martin Mclean of the University of London, Dr. Guy Thomas of the University of Basel, respectively, triggered my interest to elaborate this topic into a book. Andrea Rhyn of Basel Mission/Mission 21 helped with permission for the use of data and pictures from the Mission House in Basel. The illustrious researcher, the late Sally Chilver of Oxford, helped with pertinent German sources and Dr. Felicity Breets of the University of Sunderland did a lot of proofreading.

Dr. Nixon K. Takor, Dr. Lang and Dr. Sobse Emmanuel, all of the University of Bamenda further proofread and made useful suggestions. To N. Patrick Tata fell the assiduous task of editing this work to its final shape, capped with a befitting preface. My son, Daniel Fombit, his wife, Bernice Wakuna, with Elvira and Mildred offered my wife and I, the comfort of their homes to organise the data for final touches to the work, benefitting from Daniel's computing skill. I count myself very honoured and humbled by the splendid foreword from the Moderator of the Presbyterian Church in Cameroon, the Right Rev. Samuel Fonki.

From the Archives of the Presbyterian Church in Cameroon, the Library and Archives of the University of Ibadan, the National Archive Buea, the University of London, the Public Records Office, London and the British Library and Museum I gleaned much literature for this study. We are immensely grateful to all the officers of these institutions that served us unreservedly.

ABBREVIATIONS

BM - Basel Mission
BMC- Basel Mission College
BMS - Basel Missionary Society
CDCWU - Cameroon Development Corporation Workers Union
CPC - Cameroon Protestant College, Bali
CWU - Cameroon Welfare Union
EEC - Eglise Evangéliqe du Cameroun
ICMS - International Conference of Mission Societies
ICPM - International Council of Protestant Missions
KENU - Kamerun Ex-servicemen National Union
NNDP - Nigerian National Democratic Party
PCSC - Presbyterian Church in Southern Cameroon
PCWC - Presbyterian Church in West Cameroon
PCC - Presbyterian Church in Cameroon
PRO - Public Records Office RTC Rural Training Centres SOAS
    School of Oriental and African Studies
SJC - Sacerdotes Cordis Jesu SJC Saint Joseph's College Sase
WTTC - Women's Teacher Training College
RTC - Rural Training Centres

INTRODUCTION

In 1957, the Basel Missionary Society or *Basler Evangelische Missionsgesellschaft* (in the German language), granted independence to a locally established Church which became known as the Presbyterian Church in Southern Cameroons (PCSC) until the independence and reunification of Cameroon in 1961. This local Church was founded in the British Southern Cameroons territory where the Basel Mission had established missionary activities since 1886.

As the territory altered political status and name, the local Church also adopted new designations. Thus from 1961, when the territory became a federated state of West Cameroon, it was known as the Presbyterian Church in West Cameroon (PCWC) but in 1972 the Church was renamed Presbyterian Church in Cameroon (PCC), following the birth of the unitary state and the dissolution of the Federation in Cameroon.

In 1966, the Basel Mission handed over all the schools and educational services, which they had established and developed since their arrival in Cameroon in 1886 to the new Church. Since then the PCC has managed and expanded the school system, for the most part satisfactorily, notwithstanding stormy times. More than five decades after independence, it becomes necessary to revisit the educational efforts of the Basel Mission that laid the foundation for the PCC to contribute to the educational development of Cameroon.

Indubitably, the educational activities started by Christian Missionary Societies during the colonial period in Africa are etched in the history of Western education in Cameroon and almost all of tropical Africa indelibly. The Christians were educated and trained by these Missionary Societies. Now belonging to independent Christian churches, they have sustained and even improved upon the services of these churches. The churches currently offer comparatively better educational centres, associated with properly systematized moral education and excellent academic performance. It is proper to accede to the logical conclusion that the exceptional qualities of most of these schools bear witness to the solidity of the foundations laid by the founding fathers.

On the other hand, the inappropriateness, or rather, failure of Western education in Cameroon and Africa to enhance development, urges one to find out if the problems are not outcomes of the nature and method of the introduction of education by the Missionary Societies. For, although much has been written about the Basel Mission, little has specifically been written on their contributions to education.

The Basel Missionary Society provided education in Cameroon from 1886 to 1968 under different imperial and national regimes, specifically, the German and British colonial administrations. Following the defeat of the German imperial rule in Cameroon in the First World War, all Germans and people associated with the Germanic race were expelled from Cameroon. The territory was then partitioned between the French and the British to be administered as mandatory territories of the League of Nations till 1945. When the League of Nations was replaced by the United Nations Organization in 1946, these territories became United Nations Trusteeship territories until independence in 1961.

Post-WW1 Missionary Resumption

When the French took up temporary administration of a portion of the Cameroon territory in 1916, before the end of the war, they immediately replaced the Basel Mission there with a French Protestant Mission from Paris *(Eglise Evangélique de Paris)*. In 1957 this Parisian mission granted independence to a local Church – *Eglise Evangélique du Cameroun* (EEC). Coordinated by John Oldham, the British colonial Government entered a lengthy negotiation to get a British protestant missionary society to replace the Basel Mission in their own sector[1]. British protestant missionary societies were reluctant to take over the missionary area of another missionary society, however. The excuse is that the International Council of Protestant Missions (ICPM) had worked in synergy with one another from 1912 and did not want to disturb in the area where the other was working. Only the Roman Catholic Missionary Society (Mill Hill Missionary Society) could therefore opt to come to the territory in 1922[2]. As a result, the Basel Missionaries were allowed to resume duty in the British sector only because by 1925 the League of Nations had lifted the band on Germans to operate in their former colonies.

In the French sector, where they had operated during the German colonial administration, the Basel Mission lost all the stations. In the English sector they continued until 1957 before granting independence to the locally established Church. However, they continued administering the Educational and Medical services of the new Church until 1968 when the Presbyterian Church in West Cameroon took over Basel Mission educational activities.

H.W. Debrunner[3] holds that the Basel Missionary Society had started a very important educational work in the Gold Coast (Ghana) in the 1830s and that their experiences in Ghana impacted on their educational activities in Cameroon. This influence syncs with the Basel Mission educational aims and objectives vis-à-vis African educational needs. It is likely that the nature and practices of the Mission's educational system is responsible for some of the current African problems. And

1 IMC/BASEL MISSIONS Box 276 in SOAS, University of London; Correspondence between the British Colonial Office, British Missionary Societies, International Council of Protestant Missions and the German Missions from 1916 to 1926 are evidence of a protracted negotiation for British protestant missions to replace the Basel Mission.
2 NAB. Ba. 1922; the intervention of Lord Lugard was significant.
3 H. W. Debrunner; *A History of Christianity in Ghana*, Accra, Watersville Publishers, 1967.

perhaps the failures and successes of the post-colonial educational works of the PCC can also be attributed to the foundation laid by the Basel Mission.

Because the Basel Mission left Cameroon since 1957, many people, especially the younger generation, are not aware that such a Missionary Society was ever part of the Cameroon educational history and system. Certainly, few people are conscious of the valuable contributions that this Mission made towards the development of Cameroon. Yet, even more than other Christian Missionary Societies operating in Cameroon during the colonial period, to the Basel Mission, Cameroon as a nation remains highly indebted. Besides, the subsuming of the Basel Mission under Mission 21[4] since the year 2000 could render their contributions less evident in the future.

Among nationalist African authors, it is held that Missionaries collaborated with colonial regimes in their imperialist exploitation of the colonized. The argument is that Missionary education under colonial regimes strengthened the economic and political supremacy of the colonisers over the colonized.[5] And indeed the authoritarian structure of the colonial administration did not exclude Missionary Societies. So the Christian Missions can logically be associated with or be directly accused of implanting or upholding the notion that education and the right to rule were synonymous. At any rate, the give and take of colonizer and missionaries was intimate, making it easy to theorize that Missionary Societies pacified the colonized for the benefit of the colonizers.[6]

Such theorizing, however, leaves out a lot of detailed

---

4 In 2000, all Swiss Missionary Societies united to form Mission 21 with the Basel Mission as just one of them.

5 See M. B. Gwanfogbe, "Changing Regimes and the Development of Education in Cameroon (1886-1966)", p. 29 for the arguments raised by J.F.A. Ajayi, E.H. Berman, A. Mamoumi and J.N. Mangan on the impact of colonial education. Also see J.K. Nyerere; *Education for Self-Reliance*, Dar es Salam. 1967, p. 22.

6 J.F.A. Ajayi (ed), *The Education Process and Historiography in Contemporary Africa*, UNESCO publication, Paris, 1985; with contributions from J. Devise, A.A. Mazrui and L.T. Wago.

contraries. For one thing, the collaboration between the colonial regimes and Missionary Societies was not always cordial. The two camps differed in their perception and treatment of the colonized people, a situation that brought on disagreements and even conflicts. They disagreed on moral grounds and attitudes towards commercial activities and the nature of labour recruitment. Besides, some colonial regimes did not tolerate the presence of Missionary Societies belonging to other European nations to operate within their colonial zones of influence.

That the Basel Mission survived under different colonial regimes (Germans, British and post-colonial national Government) in Cameroon and handed over their educational services only in 1968 to an independent Cameroonian Church becomes an issue of interest. Brazen animosity characterized the relationships between the Germans and the British and French allies, who took over colonial rule in Cameroon after the First World War. The Basel Mission and its status in this zone of conflicts of interests excite scholarly curiosity at several levels. Thus Basel Mission contributions (vis-à-vis such multifaceted circumstances) to the development of education in Cameroon craves assessment; and just how the Mission survived under those regimes, which had such widely differing perspectives, also becomes a research focus.

Much has been written about the Basel Mission evangelical activities and mention is constantly being made to its educational input when the social services are considered. For example, S. N. Shu[7] (1972) analyses the policy of collaboration between Government and voluntary agencies from 1910 to 1931. His work illuminates the differences between the three colonial regimes and the Missionary societies. But his study ended in 1931, whereas the Mission's work in education continued until 1968. W. Keller[8] (1969) makes an impressive remark on the contribution of the

---

7   S.N. Shu, *Landmarks in Cameroon Education*, Limbe, NOOREMAC Press, 1985.
8   W. Keller, *The History of the Presbyterian Church in West Cameroon*, Victoria, Pressbook, 1969.

Basel Mission to Cameroon education. However, education not being his exclusive focus, receives little analysis. In 1980, E. Madiba[9] published yet another important study that alludes to the role of the Basel Mission in the development of education in Cameroon. His bent is the inter-cultural history of Christianity and the effects of colonialism and evangelisation on education up to 1956. Madiba does not solely concentrate on the Basel Mission, and also leaves out the last decade of Basel Mission educational efforts in Cameroon (1956 to 1968).

It is Jonas Dah who comes closer home in his thesis on "Missionary Motivations and Methods."[10] He evaluates Basel Mission activities in Cameroon from 1886 to 1914. He focuses on the German colonial era in his analytical evaluation of the contribution and objectives of the Basel Mission to education. This leaves the rest of the Basel Mission educational activities unexplored.

During the Silver Jubilee of the Presbyterian Church in Cameroon in 1982, Eugene Ekiti (then Education Secretary of the Church) paid tribute to the Basel Mission for laying a good educational foundation on which the Presbyterian Church in Cameroon had to thrive. This is a situation where the entire coverage would be expected, but his context is too cursory to do justice to the weight of the contribution of the Mission to the development of education in Cameroon. Jean Van-Slageren[11] studies the *Eglise Evangélique du Cameroun* (EEC), making pertinent allusions to the valuable contributions of the Basel Mission, especially during the German period. His remarks are side comments of his central focus on the origins and development of the EEC.

An earlier study bearing on the Basel Mission educational contribution to the development of education in Cameroon was

9   E. Madiba, *Colonisation et Évangélisation en Afrique: L' héritage scolaire au Cameroun (1885-1956)*, Bern, Editions Peter Lang; 1980.
10 J. N. Dah, "Missionary Motivations and Methods: A critical examination of the Basel Mission in Cameroon, 1885-1914" PhD, Basel, 1983.
11 J. Van Slagaren, *Les origines de l' Église Évangélique du Cameroun: Mission Européennes et Christianisme Autochtone*, Leiden, E. J. Brill, 1972.

made by R. Raaflaub,[12] himself an insider who sacrificed more than two decades of his life in that service. He examines the Basel Mission relations with the state and the public in the provision of schools up to 1948, long before the period of nationalism and independence, which could have furthered understanding of the nature of collaboration between the church and the state, as well as an understanding of the reactions of Cameroonians to Missionary education.

From the above findings, it is clear that no comprehensive study specifically addresses the contributions of the Basel Mission to the evolution of education in Cameroon. That is the gap that this study sets out to fill, establishing (for comparative reasons) its findings from the fact that education under German or British rule was almost entirely the affair of Missionary Societies – a sharp contrast with the present, when the government centrally controls education. Measuring one practice against the other exposes the more effective of the two practices.

The Basel Mission is historically important, being one of only two Missionary Societies (the other being the American Presbyterian Mission) that spanned and survived the entire period of colonial rule, except for the hiatus straddling 1914 and 1925, when all German Missionaries were expelled from Cameroon upon Germany's defeat in World War I. This German Missionary Society survived and contributed to the growth of education in Cameroon even in an atmosphere of passionate animosity between the Germans and the Anglo-French alliance.

Demonstrably, education was at the forefront of Basel Mission evangelizing success in Cameroon, even while the unfriendly French-English colonial setting prevailed. The successors of the Basel Missionaries in Cameroon, (PCC) and Mission 21, which has replaced the Basel Mission, need to be abreast of the strategies that their predecessors applied to surmount problems in education.

---

12 F. Raaflaub, "Gebt uns Lehrer, Geschichte und Gegenwartsaufgabe der Basler Mission Kamerun", PhD Basel, 1948.

The PCC archives, the Basel Mission house in Switzerland, data from the national archives in Buea, Yaoundé, Ibadan (Nigeria), SOAS Library, University of London, and the Public Records Office (PRO) in London provide the primary material for this study. Focal theses, journals, and books corroborate the primary sources. The present study is broadly framed, with focus on the period under the Germans covering the earlier section while the later section spans 1914-1966, expounding on the British presence, occasionally impinged upon by French interests.

CHAPTER ONE

BASEL MISSION EDUCATION UNDER GERMAN COLONIAL ADMINISTRATION

The British Baptist Missionary Society operated in the territory of Cameroon from 1842 and was replaced in 1886 by the Basel Mission that came at the behest of the German government to participate in Cameroon's educational development until 1968. The choice of this Mission was urged on by political manoeuvres arising from the intense nationalistic chauvinism of German colonialism. German colonial enthusiasts, whether in political or economic circles, felt that German Protestants were more patriotic and so better able to implant German culture and influence in the newly acquired colonies.

They appealed to the experienced Basel Mission to apply knowledge acquired from earlier activities in India, the Gold Coast and in the Far East to establish German colonial culture in Cameroon. But the Lutheran revivalist spirit of the Basel Mission and their rigid adherence to Christian ethics was doomed to inhibit imperialistic collaboration with the German colonial government. The Basel Mission was determined to protect the indigenous people, which inevitably generated disagreements with the colonialist spirit of economic exploitation and nationalistic egoism. Tensions and confrontations between the Basel Mission and the German Colonial Government over educational developments were thus written on the canvas of their divergent interests.

Any meaningful analysis of the contributions of the Basel Mission to Cameroon education has, for this reason, to take into account several factors: the origins and objectives of the Mission, their worldviews, the background of the Missionaries and their relationships with the Government and the people of Cameroon, the relationship between the Field Missionaries and the Home Board, as well as with the other Missionary Societies.

BM Background and Choice

The Basel Mission Society was derived from a flourishing cooperation between pietistic groups in the German speaking cantons of Basel in Switzerland and the Germans of Wurttemburg. This relationship in itself was the result of a common religious background based on pietism. Erik Hallden[13] intimates that pietism was supported by pastors to survive in the national and cantonal churches of Wurttemburg and Basel, and that the seriousness attached to the study of theology and pietism gradually gave them a footing in the universities of Basel and Tubingen. These interrelations and affiliations were crowned in 1780 by the establishment of *Deutsche Gesellschaaft zur Beforderung reiner Lehre und Wahrer Gottselligkeit* (the German society for the furtherance of pure learning and true spirituality). Basel was the headquarters of this society because its legislation favoured free evangelical movements, which honest persons of all classes supported. It was from this Christian Society that in 1815 the Evangelical Mission of Basel (the Basel Mission) was born. Basel then became the bridge between the German and Swiss members. German colonial administration preferred the Basel Mission in its colony to other Missionary Societies, considering it best representative of German interests.

The Calvinistic background of the Basel Mission influenced it to conceptualize religious, social and national life as one. Calvinism required not merely individual good deeds but the whole life of its devotees to express a system of piety in action. Thus, with the involvement of religious leaders, educated people and

---

13 Erik Hallden, *The Culture Policy of the Basel Mission in the Cameroons, 1886-1905*, Lund, 1968.

pious business people, the Basel Mission could be viewed as systematically serving the spiritual needs of the people, satisfying their social needs, and also extending enlightenment to the less privileged.

The nature of collaboration between Missionary societies and the German Government was hotly debated at the beginning of German colonial rule. The intention of the German Government was to direct German Missionary societies to diffuse German culture - *Kulturarbeit*.[14] It was suspicious of foreign nationals who might be opposed or indifferent to its imperial interests. Yet the missions were not a unified perspective, for some Missions welcomed this appeal while others resisted.

The Basel Mission Society could not yield to these pressures. For one thing, it was not wholly German. As earlier stated, it was a product of protestant scholasticism and evangelical pietism that had evolved from the Church Reformation. The ideas of the Mission were also influenced by the liberal rationalism of the age of enlightenment (*Aufklärung*). Besides, despite its bonds with Württemburg, Basel did not join the rest of the German states when they unified in 1871. And remaining international (with Swiss and German leadership), it could not totally yield to German colonial pressures.

BM and Colonial Collaboration

The Basel Mission's spiritual roots lay in the Protestantism of the early nineteenth century revivalism, which opposed political involvement, particularly the scramble for colonies. So, German colonial interests were not a Basel Mission project. And the lower middle-class origin of most Missionaries inclined them to indifferent conservatism rather than political adventures. They also found refuge in the staunch arguments raised by Gustav Warneck (1834-1910), a reputable theologian and teacher of German protestant Missionaries of the period. Warneck opposed

---

14 H.W. Gensichen, "Evangelisation and Civilisation: The Germans" in *International Bulletin of Missionary Research*, No. 6, 1982. p. 52.

the nationalistic inclinations of Missionaries and considered Mission work an international task to be respected by all, including the German Reich. He opposed the rendering of service to the German Empire at the expense of service to God.

The majority of German Protestants upheld Warneck's views, but a faction was influenced by Friedrich Fabri (1824-1891), another important theologian. Fabri considered colonies as solutions to German socioeconomic and political problems and missionary work a junior partner in national undertakings.

Those Missionaries who had earlier encouraged German colonialism advocated for the Fabri faction, implying collaboration with the Government. In 1885, they expressed their views at the sixth conference of German Protestant Missions in Bremen. They blamed the shortcomings of their Missionary work on lack of colonial Government support. To them, the Mission and the colonial regime were bound to bring about greater success if they belonged to the same nationality.

In view of these differing perspectives then, it is no wonder that the nature and pattern of Mission collaboration became a major issue at the Bremen conference of German Protestant Missions in 1885. For the majority, missionary and colonialist objectives, though culturally similar, were diametrically opposed in methods of achievement. They only concurred over civilizing objectives. And in that respect, it was argued that, without evangelical contributions, the civilizing objective of colonialism was incomplete. The role of Mission schools to cultivate loyal, obedient and conscientious citizens in the colonies was considered of utmost importance to colonial development.[15]

Apart from German South West Africa (Namibia) and Togoland (Togo), there were no missionary societies in German colonies at the time of the 1885 conference. Yet general opinion favoured German Missions in German colonies. Since the Basel Mission was in the Gold Coast from 1828, the consensus

---

15 More on the nature of Mission collaboration with colonial government can be seen in E. Hallden, op. cit.

was for them to establish in Cameroon, to replace the British Baptist Missionary Society, which had been there since 1844.

FIGURE 1.1. Julius von Soden, First German Governor of Cameroon (1885-1891)

Further pressure came from Von Soden, first German colonial Governor of Cameroon (1885- 1891), and from the management of the Woerman Company in Cameroon, which was established before the German annexation. Adolf Woermann, who was a business magnet from Hamburg and the leader of the Woerman Company, convinced German Chancellor Otto Von Bismarck to extend imperial protection over the region. Thus business motives strongly influenced Germany to colonize Cameroon,[16] which explains why the likes of Woerman opposed the presence of the British Baptist Missionary Society in Cameroon, the latter belonging to a rival European country with rival business designs.

16 V. T. LeVine's *The Cameroons from Mandate to Independence*, UCL, 1964.

This nationalistic antagonism was not the only difficulty, for the missions themselves had restrictions in choosing to take up mission. The head of the Basel Mission delegation at the Bremen Conference, Theodor Oehler, had received instructions from the Basel Mission Home Board to decline the invitation to operate in Cameroon because of the Mission's financial situation and unwillingness to offend the British Baptist Missionary Society. However, the Board advised him to accept it, if the majority of the participants favoured the choice of the Basel Mission to replace the British Baptists. Oehler eventually accepted the decision of the conference on three conditions: first, he asked for financial assistance. Next, he requested a clear approval from the British Baptist Missionary Society so as to clear up allegations of rivalry and also required the approval of the German colonial regime in Cameroon in order to elude any eventual accusations. Lastly, he informed the conference that the Basel Mission's final decision to go to Cameroon would depend on the approval of both German and Swiss authorities within the Mission.

BM and the British Baptist Missionary Society

The unwillingness of the Basel Mission to offend the British Baptist Missionary Society in taking over the Cameroon Mission field is a point for clarification. Undoubtedly, the British Baptist Missionary Society that provided education since 1844 was not willing to continue under German rule. For the new political dispensation, following German annexation complicated their plans. Not least of the complications, was the introduction of the German language, compounded by such undesirable factors as financial limitations, a high death rate of Missionaries resulting from tropical diseases, and the demands for more manpower and attention in the 1878 newly-started Mission field in the Congo. They were thus as disposed to hand over Cameroon to a German Missionary Society as the German colonial Government in Cameroon was unwilling to continue with them (British Baptists) – having indeed sent a representative to declare their preference for the Basel Mission at the conference of German protestant Missions.

The German imperial government had further reason to prefer the Basel Mission. For, shortly after the declaration of German colonial rule in Cameroon, the people of Douala not only resented but actually revolted against it in December 1884, a revolt which imperial Germany interpreted as a manipulation of the Baptist Missionary Society. And indeed, some form of evidence for this suspicious bent could be concocted from the fact that the British Baptist Mission had masterminded letters inviting Queen Victoria to annex Cameroon.

The rivalry between the Germans and the English preceding the annexation was an important factor too, with Victoria which had been established in 1858 by the British Baptists featuring prominently. The Baptists refused to hand over Victoria to the Germans on grounds that it was their personal property; this, in spite of the fact that the British Government was compelled to recognize German annexation of Cameroon during the Berlin Conference. Asked to negotiate with the Germans on how to quit the town, the Baptists had their pound of flesh to take, and asked for 3000 pound sterling,[17] which then was a colossal amount of money. It was partly because of this dilemma posed by the Victoria saga that the German Government preferred a protestant missionary body such as the Basel Mission to lead the negotiations with the British Baptists (since in principle British Baptists were affiliates of the protestant body).

Following these pressures, the Basel Mission sent an exploratory team to Cameroon from the 11th to 28th January 1886 comprising Rittman and Bonner, who were at the time Basel Missionaries in the Gold Coast (Ghana) and Rev. Binetsch, who represented the North German Missionary Society. On their return, the Basel Mission team submitted an encouraging report and in June 1886, the Basel Mission formally applied to the Foreign Office to establish in Cameroon.

Since the German imperial Government was anxious to have

---

17 W. Keller; op. cit. p.1 1.

them in Cameroon, an immediate approval was granted to all that the Basel Mission asked for. The German Government and the West African German Commercial Syndicate, which included Woerman, promised them support. With this political backing and promise for financial sustenance, the Basel Mission established in Cameroon. The conference had established a good atmosphere for collaboration within which the Mission's ambitions were guaranteed and the political objectives of the imperial regime were secured. Thus, both had to work together. The recognition of the Basel Mission at the conference gave it a more German character. Implicitly then, the Basel Mission was given responsibility for Germany's new colonial situation because, although the Mission's headquarters was in Basel-Switzerland, the Missionary Society had a German branch at Stuttgart, which gave it a German identity and helped to attract German financing.

Such then was the background of the Basel Mission and why the German imperial government chose it. The Basel Mission had useful experience in colonial ventures in India, the Gold Coast (Ghana) and in the Far East and thus was better than any German Mission. The German colonial administrators attributed the Cameroonian resistance to their administration to the influence of the British Baptist Missionaries, making it necessary to replace them with a German Mission. The West African German Commercial Syndicate led by Woerman was also influential in establishing the Basel Mission in Cameroon for the safety of their business. The stage was thus set for the arrival of the Basel Mission in Cameroon and the commencement of their contribution to the development of education in the country.

CHAPTER TWO

SETTING UP BASEL MISSION EDUCATION IN CAMEROON

Before taking possession of the Mission field in Cameroon, the Basel Mission paid £3,000 for the land and property taken over from the British Baptist Missionary Society which was located at the time only in Douala and Victoria. This compensation done with, the first contingent of Missionaries arrived Cameroon on 23rd December 1886, comprising the Rev. Gottlieb Munz and his wife, the Rev. Christian Dilger, the Rev. Johannes Bizer, and the Rev. Friederich Becher – the latter unfortunately died on arrival. Because of his experience in working with Africans in the Gold Coast from 1880 to 1883, Rev. Gottlieb Munz was made the first Field Secretary of the Basel Mission in Cameroon, i.e., the head of the Mission's operation in the territory.

The Basel Mission inherited four schools with 368 pupils from the outgoing British Baptist Missionaries. There was an elementary school in Bethel (Douala) and there were Vernacular Schools located at Victoria, Bakundu-Banga and Mungo, all with problems of staffing and proper supervision.

Although the British Baptist Missionaries already translated the Bible into Douala, the English language was the dominant medium of instruction. The Basel Mission was determined to extend their educational and evangelical activities not only within the coastal towns as their predecessors, but also into the hinterland in any language, so long as it enhanced the propagation of the Gospel.

Problems of Expansion

The expected rapid expansion was inhibited by some initial problems. Firstly, denominational differences, especially in doctrinal and administrative systems, caused disagreements between the newly-arrived Basel Mission and the Cameroonian members of the departed British Baptist Church. One major source of discord was the baptismal ritual. The Basel Mission preferred sprinkling but the Baptists opted for immersion in water. The Basel Mission advocated for child baptism while the Baptists argued that only grownup persons able to reason should receive baptism. At the level of administration, the Basel Mission preferred uniting all their congregations and having a central administration while the Baptists practised the independence of individual congregations.

And it is not as if the Basel Mission had no basis for running the mission, for the Baptist Missionaries had reached an agreement with them that clearly stipulated that Cameroonian members of the British Baptist Mission were to operate under the Basel Mission.

The disagreements led to a split as the local Baptist Christians led by Pastors Joshua Dibundi and George Nkwe declared themselves members of an autonomous "Native Baptist Church". This declaration marked the beginning of the **Native Baptist Church** in Cameroon that thrives to this day. The secession encouraged the Basel Mission to expand into the hinterland to plough new fields and imbued their own adherents with their own doctrine.

The attempt to expand, however, brought them face-to-face with another challenge and which was to last throughout their Missionary years in Cameroon – the Roman Catholic Mission. Under Father Heinrich Vieter, the Roman Catholics arrived and started missionary work in Cameroon in 1890. Thereafter, the two Missionary Societies competed for pupils and Christian followers.

The Reichstag meeting of November 1885 had given the Basel Mission the impression that the German Government did not want the Roman Catholic Mission in Cameroon. This was largely because the Catholic Missionary Societies applying at the time were not of German origin. Such was the nationalistic chauvinism that enthused colonialism in the second half of the 19th century, and was to eventually bring about the First World War. Coupled with the Franco-German colonial rivalry, the German Government dithered for five years to authorize a Catholic Mission in Cameroon. They finally accepted, when the Vatican decided to send a German-based Catholic Mission called the Pallotine Fathers.

These initial difficulties, combined with the rough tropical climate, the difficult terrain, as well as resistance from some Cameroonians, conditioned the nature of the development of Basel Mission evangelical and educational effort in Cameroon at the beginning of the German colonial rule.

BM Educational Objectives

The Basel Mission had a twofold objective for education. Firstly, they aimed at evangelizing and converting young Cameroonians who went to school into Christianity, and through them, reach their heathen parents. The Mission's leaders, such as Oehler, held the view that schools were the best way of influencing the population and winning converts into Christianity. The second objective was to produce educated African assistants (*Gehilfen*). These would eventually become Christian leaders (catechists, pastors, teachers, clerks, artisans, technicians) for both church and state. The two objectives were complementary; both aimed ultimately at establishing the Church. In 1888, the Field Secretary, Rev. Munz, stated that the school system had to help them to raise educated assistants. It was expected that every convert would be able to read the Bible and the society would be permeated with Christian ideals. To achieve these aims, the Mission was determined to use local languages. Douala became the medium of instruction in the schools of the Forest Region and Bali (Mungaka) which was the language of their first station in the Western Grassfields, became the educational and evangelical language of the Grassfields.

Experiences from Mission fields in India, China and the Gold Coast came to good use as they re-organised the inherited schooling system. Initial schooling lasted four years; the first two years emphasizing reading, writing and arithmetic in the vernacular. In the third year, German was introduced. In the fourth year, Geography and History were added. But in all the classes, Religious Instruction had priority. The first school to undergo this reform was Bethel. There the first German literate Douala people got education, including Rudolf Douala Manga Bell, who later became king of the Douala people and Ngosso Din.

Organization of BM Schools

Initially, the schools were founded, organized and administered by missionaries in their respective stations as need arose. The school was a social necessity through which the missionaries could have contact with the youths so as to prepare them for the service of the Church and colonial administration. Because schools primarily served as a means for evangelization, the need for central control was not immediately expressed.

The missionary was the highest school hierarchy in any given mission school, although he had to make reports to the Mission School Inspector who in turn submitted a report to the Home Board in Basel. The Mission School Inspector was the highest school authority in Cameroon.

The Head teacher administered the school, often assisted by the Evangelist. The local authorities (Cameroonians), deemed uninformed in matters of education, were hardly ever consulted. However, where the local language such as Douala or Mungaka had to be used, they occasionally consulted some of the local authorities on matters of language accuracy.

With time it became necessary for the Basel Mission to structure an organized school system. They opened various types of schools to accomplish the objectives of their school system. But, for all the efforts, it was a poor start, lacking a central coordination of the individual efforts of the respective Missionaries in parishes. Compounding this disarray, were makeshift rival undertakings even among fellow Basel Mission parishes. But the height of rivalry was generated by other Christian denominations who were also offering education. The consequence was a spate of hastily opened schools in a bid to outdo the rivals in the number of converts gained. This foolhardy expansionism went counter to managerial ability, for catastrophic shortage of the required number of qualified teachers to cope with the enrolments was glaring at all the rush in the face. They quickly fangled some training of some people to both teach and serve as catechists. These teachers-cum-catechists hardly imbibed or possessed more than very basic knowledge of reading and writing. Alas, these were those who had to teach as well as administer some schools. The quality of their input is anybody's quick guess. And yet numbers could be invoked to argue for progress. It was easy to show how the number of schools had grown more than thirty-threefold, rising from a mere four in 1888 to 133 by 1898. Enrolment too could be quoted to have grown about tenfold from 368 to 3,278 within the decade. As it looked, the growth was phenomenal, but with it came great challenges that obliged the Basel Mission to make structural reform. It decided that there were to be four types of schools, corresponding to their new-fangled terms of reference or demands.

Four School Types

1. *Vernacular or Village / Bush Schools*

Vernacular or village schools originated from the desire to teach the pupils in their local or village language and not in the German or European language. In the Coastal and Forest areas the Basel Mission used the Douala language for the village schools. In the Grassfields area, they used the Bali Language (*Mungaka*) for the village schools. These schools offered three years of education under a teacher-catechist. Centrally, the teaching comprised a general Christian education of the pupils as a basis on which the Christian community would eventually be established. Village Schools, which the colonial administration eventually derogatively referred to as Bush Schools, were very popular, being schools for everybody.

Not having buildings for these schools, they initially operated in the court-yards of chiefs' palaces or in church buildings. Those who taught there were almost invariably also in charge of the local congregations as catechists and evangelists. Here, pupils were taught to recognise the advantages of Christian culture as against the evils of their indigenous traditions. The snag was worsened by the poor quality training and scant education received by these so-called teachers-cum-catechists, which made their transmission of knowledge ineffective. Evidence of this bleak fact is that the pupils became neither complete Christians nor did they maintain their African cultures. A careful examination of the state of teaching and doctrinal practices reveals jumbled syncretism. This was more glaringly brought out as the common practice and mindset during the non-missionary days, following the expulsion of the Missionaries upon the defeat of the Germans in Cameroon during WWI as discussed in chapter five below.

2. Boys' / Middle Schools

All Basel Mission stations, except Victoria, had a central school, referred to as a Boys' School (*Knabenschule*) or Middle School (*Mittelschule*). The best graduates of the village schools were admitted here through competitive entrance examinations. Boys' Schools therefore had pupils from several villages and since some of them came from far off distances, a boarding system was established. Initially, individual pupils were responsible for their own feeding but eventually, a communal feeding system was established. Food was produced from school farms and gardens worked by the pupils themselves because the pupils practiced agriculture, which was one of their school subjects.

Within ten years from 1895, some six of these schools were set up in various points in the mission fields. The first of these Boys' School was opened at Lobetal in 1895, the second at Buea in 1896 by Rev. Bizer, the third in Mangamba in 1898, and a fourth opened at Edea in 1899 was transferred to Lobatel in 1901. In 1902, the Village Schools in Nyasoso and Bombe were also transformed into Boys' Schools and in 1905, Sakbayeme Village School, along River Sanaga was also transformed into a Boys' School.

FIGURE 2.1. Basel Mission School, Buea

The study course in Boys' Schools covered two years and the local language was used, although German was introduced. Most pupils continued their studies to this level in order to acquire the German language which was required for employment, in either the Government or private company service. After the two years' course, the brightest boys were selected and sent to Middle Schools. Since there was a keen competition with the Catholics and Baptists for the provision of good quality education, Basel Mission Middle Schools were also quickly multiplied.

Pupils graduating from Mangamba continued their Middle School education at Bonaberi while those from Bombe and Nyasoso went to the Middle School in Buea and those from Sakbayeme were sent to Lobetal Middle school. This practice continued until 1912.

Middle Schools offered three-year courses, and because of the distances from which the pupils came, they were, inevitably, boarding schools. But unlike Village Schools staffed by only one European and several Africans, Middle Schools had two Europeans and other Africans. The local language continued to be used at this level, but German was allocated six hours of lessons a week. Other subjects included Arithmetic, History, Geography, and Literacy in the local language (Douala or Mungaka), Religious instruction, besides such practical subjects as basketry, book-keeping, baking and agriculture.

Middle Schools did not only prepare people for employment in the lower ranks of the colonial administration and in private business companies; they were also centres for training teacher-catechists for village stations. Until 1898, they were the highest level of learning in the Basel Mission school system. Pupils who could not continue at the end of the first year were usually recruited by their former station managers as teacher-catechists. Middle schools supplied the most educated graduates of the time and enjoyed colonial support because of the desire for the diffusion of the German language.

3. *German Schools (Deutsche Schulen)*[18]

The increasing demand for Cameroonians in the lower ranks of the colonial administration and in private business enterprises led the Basel Mission to operate two schools, specifically to prepare graduates for these services. They were known as German Schools because of the emphasis on the German language and were located at Bonabela and at Bonanjo in Douala. This system of schooling was copied from the Government school at Bonabela when Governor Puttkamer handed it over to the Basel Mission in 1897. Both the Bonanjo and Bonabela schools were different from all other Basel Mission schools in both conceptions

---

18 Basel Mission A.E-2.16; Kamerun 1903, Report by Stutz and Diebol on the German school in Bonanjo.

and aims. They produced graduates that were esteemed for the colonial administration.

The curriculum comprised German language studies, the history and geography of Germany, and special training towards appointment into the colonial administration or commercial firms. Although some Missionaries questioned the value of such an educational system to the Mission, it was defended that the Mission would have adherents in Government jobs and commercial companies in order to have reliable people in these sectors that could come to their assistance in time of need. The graduates were often considered too young and insufficiently prepared for those jobs, however. Other shortcomings of this schooling system included the frequent transfers of the German teachers and the inability of their Cameroonian counterparts to teach the German language efficiently. They thus often lacked qualified staff and school equipment, in addition to the fact that the scramble for admissions in the school system far outstripped the available places.

These three types of schooling offered by the Basel Mission soon demanded a fourth type. For, to establish and develop these schools effectively, the Mission needed to meet the acute shortage of staff by creating a training centre for teachers.

4. Helpers' School (Gehilfenschule)

Helpers' Schools were established to train teacher/catechists as school assistants. Graduates from this school were to serve as teachers in schools and catechists in congregations. It was equally to enable the Mission to prepare Cameroonian Christians who could eventually take over Church and educational responsibilities. The first *Gehilfenschule* was opened at Bonaku in 1889. In order to prepare the future Church leaders, the Mission was determined to apply Henry Venn's concept of the "three self" principle in the training. The principle required locally established churches to become "self-supporting, self-governing and self-propagating." To emphasize this point, Oehler had insisted that all churches founded by the Mission had to be prepared in such a way that they should not depend on external aid. In other words, they had to be systematized to be self-sufficiently sustainable.

The school system was developed and controlled by the Mission with little or no intervention from the Government until 1910. An earlier attempt to seek Mission-Government collaboration by Theodore Christaller (the first German Government teacher) was abandoned when he died in 1894. When Governor Puttkamer requested Bohner, the superintendent of Basel Mission (1889-1897), to propose an education system for the territory in 1897, Bohner suggested that Government could either establish a complete education system with inspection service and teacher training or leave education entirely to the Missions.[19] It is therefore evident that the Basel Mission played an unquestionably important role in education under the German colonial rule.[20]

BM Education Problems and Reform Attempts

Although the introduction of Western education in Cameroon was rightly that of the British Baptist Missionary Society, its expansion and propagation particularly during the German rule was greatly that of the Basel Mission. The Baptist Missionary Society had provided education only to a handful of people in Douala and Victoria – coastal commercial towns. They only had local chiefs and the coastal people to react to their activities, but with no rival missionary societies or foreign domination to interfere in their work.

Upon the arrival of the Basel Mission, colonial rule was already established. The German imperial government soon went back on the open latitude promised the Basel Mission before their acceptance to replace the Baptists, first, by letting in the Roman Catholic Mission. Next, the colonial administration soon insisted on the Mission obeying imperialist demands.

---

19 BMA.E-2.10; Kamerun 1897, Curriculum in Mission Secondary schools.
20 Statistics in Table 2 further justify this statement.

This exposed the Basel Mission to a wide range of problems, compounded by the fact that they were facing both negative and positive reactions from Cameroonians of all shades of life, rivalry from other Missionary Societies of both Protestant and Catholic origins, and were not allowed to work within Muslim areas of the Cameroon territory. Restrictions from the German regime added to these as well as internal problems erupting from disagreements between individual missionaries. There were also frequent interferences from the Home Board of the Mission. But worse, like all other Europeans, the missionaries suffered from tropical diseases, especially malaria. The stacks of problems were no doubt injurious to their work, affecting their provision of education to Cameroonians.

What also might not have looked like an issue from missionary perspectives was the significant problem that affected all Missionary enterprises at the time – European perception of Africans. African culture was considered inherently bedevilled by evils, including polygamy, bride-price, slavery and superstition. The Missionaries, who could not extricate themselves from their European culture, believed that any meaningful educational policy must aim at eradicating these dark forces.

Such a policy could not go unchallenged by Africans. The missions have to be ascribed blame for downgrading the traditions of Africans. They might indeed be exempted from the economic and political determinisms of imperialism. They might indeed be exonerated from the emphasis on the universalities of the educational mechanisms by which the economically and politically dominant groups of the colonizing society generalized their power on the colonial stage. But by their Eurocentric interpretation of African values, they served as the lackeys of imperialism. They shared with the colonial regimes the establishment of debilitating psychological factors through the social arrangements prevailing then and to which they fully or partially subscribed. They induced types of child-training practices which fostered personalities characterized by marked feelings of dependency and inferiority. Then, too, they exposed the African only to such educational and cultural stimuli that tended to erase the significance of the African past. By both the limitations of curriculum and teaching method, the African was over-exposed to selected elements of the metropolitan culture.

Such were the problems that the Basel Mission faced – intricate and multiple. A prime-moving impetus was, however, the rivalry from other missionary activities.

Rival Missionary Societies

1. *The American Presbyterian Missionary Society*

Even before the English Baptist Missionary Society left the country, the American Presbyterian Missionary Society was working in the Batanga area. They entered the country through the south, coming from the Congo where French colonial rule restricted their activities. In 1888, they requested for formal permission from the German colonial administration and effectively started work in 1890. Rudin argues that their major problem was that of language. The German administration insisted on the use of the German language but they continued with English. With leaders like Dr. Good and Dr. Johnston, they occupied the Bulu land, extending to Elat, Lolodorf, Kribi, Yaoundé and others. By 1914, they had 243 schools with 16,697 pupils.

2. *The Roman Catholic Mission (Pallotine Missionary Society and Sacred Heart Fathers)*

As stated earlier, education was designed and provided by the Christian Missions until 1910. The German colonial administration policy restricted the different Missions to operate only in specific geographical areas. While this was generally respected by the Protestant Missions, the Roman Catholic Mission argued that geographical restriction contradicted Christ's commission to teach all men.

It is important to note that the Roman Catholic Missions were even more interested to work in Cameroon when the Germans annexed the country than were the Protestant Missionary

Societies. As early as June 1885, Rev. Father Weik of the French Catholic organization, (*Congregation du St. Esprit et du St. Coeur de Marie*) had expressed the desire to see Otto Von Bismarck for permission to work in Cameroon. The German government was ready to permit them to establish in Cameroon but gave them restrictive conditions.
1. That they should be ready to work in a separate area from that of the Protestants.
2. That they must use the German language.
3. That they had to fly the German flag.

These conditions were too difficult for the French Catholic Mission to fulfil. In 1889, the German Pallotine Mission, founded by Cardinal Palloti who died earlier (1850), once again requested to work in Cameroon. The regime accepted the appeal of the Mission on condition that they did not interfere in the areas in which the Protestant Missionaries were engaged. They were also asked to use the German language in the Mission field. When the German colonial administration sought the opinion of the Basel Mission in 1890, the Basel Mission declared that they had no objection, if the Roman Catholics worked in Cameroon, but requested that the government should avoid Catholic interference with their own work. And so the Pallotine Mission led by Father Heinrich Vieter, who previously served in Brazil, started operating in Cameroon with 13 people in 1890. By 1913 they already had 93 European Missionaries and 12,532 pupils in 151 schools. Unavoidably however, there were bound to eventually have disagreements but not such conflicts as would affect the progress and expansion of their respective missionary work.

In 1912, the Sacred Heart Mission (a new Catholic Mission) was assigned the Adamawa area which included the Western Highlands. That year, they founded stations in Shisong (in Kumbo) and Njinikom, led by F.J. Lennartz. The Shisong Missionaries belonged to the Sacerdotes Cordis Jesu (S.C.J.), also referred to as the Dehonians, after the founder, Mgr. Dehon. The school in Shisong had 100 pupils and the other stations were just starting when the First World War broke out.

3. The Native Baptist Church and the German Baptist Missionary Society

On taking over the work started by the British Baptist Missionary Society in Cameroon in 1886, the Basel Mission had accepted to absorb their Cameroonian Christians. Even though the British Baptists had arranged beforehand for the right of the indigenous Christians to continue the Baptist denominational traditions, the Basel Mission did not take long to divulge fundamental doctrinal and administrative differences that affected the union. These disparities led the indigenous Baptist Christians to discontinue worshiping with the Basel Mission; they declared themselves the *Native* Baptists i.e. the Cameroonian Christian followers of the British Baptist Church. Schlatter suggests that the Basel Mission felt that the British Baptist Missionaries had given their indigenous Cameroon Christians too much independence and self-government in their religious organization. This argument has been supported by Harry Rudin who opines that the indigenous Cameroonian Baptists separated from the Basel Mission not because of doctrinal differences but rather on account of church organization and discipline. Whatever the causes, the disagreement resulted in the establishment of the Native Baptist Church from 1889, led by Pastors Joshua Dibundi and George Nkwe.

4. The German Baptist Mission

The Native Baptist Church functioned like any other Missionary Society and had its own schools. Initially, they intended to have only Cameroonians to head their church. After a short experience of complete independence, the Native Baptists expressed a desire to have a European Baptist Missionary Society as their sponsor. In 1889, one of their Christians known as Alfred Bell, then studying in Germany, appealed to a German Congregation of Baptist Christians to come to the relief of the Native Baptist Church. He entreated the congregation with a pathetic narration of the schism between the Basel Mission and the local Baptist Christians in Cameroon that took place in 1888. According to C. W. Weber, this request evoked the sympathy of German Baptists and on its behest a German Baptist Mission, a branch of the American Baptist Mission started in 1890, was dispatched to Cameroon in 1891. However, although it was a German Baptist Mission, the majority of the missionaries, including their pioneer leader, August Steffens, were actually Americans, albeit of German origins.

The German Baptist Mission arrived in Cameroon when, as recorded by R. Donat, the Native Baptist Church had 442 communicant members, two schools and 634 pupils. They worked together until 1897 when friendly relations proved almost impossible and the Native Baptist Christians had to separate. A conflict of authority had developed between Suvern of the German Baptist Missionaries and Joshua Dibundi, the leader of the Native Baptist Church.

The German Baptist Missionary enterprise was therefore affected by this initial problem. However, by 1914, they had 57 elementary schools with an enrolment of 3,151 pupils in six main stations with 40 European missionaries. They also had three post-elementary schools in Douala and a middle school for boys and another for girls.

These were the Missionary Societies operating schools in Cameroon under the German regime. The rivalry for Christians through the provision of schools by these Christian Missions sometimes resulted in frictions that affected the school system. The absence of a centralized education policy to guide the functioning of schools, and the absence of concerted forums involving all the Missions, equally resulted in conflicting school systems set up by the respective Missions. The curricula, timetables, duration of school cycles, language of instruction, etc., were different from one Christian Mission to the other and even from one parish to the other within the same Missionary Society.

In 1907, the German imperial government thought it necessary to reform education and therefore called for the first education conference involving all education providers in the territory. The conference did not provide solutions to educational problems. Until 1910, confusion continued to reign in education. Even within the individual Missions, there was chaos as respective Missionaries offered different programmes in their parishes with makeshift attempts by individual Missions to address problems. Each Missionary Society had to reform its own education system.

Internal Hurdles of BM Education Reforms

The Basel Mission attempts to reform education in Cameroon were often hindered by internal disagreement either among the field Missionaries or between the field Missionaries and the Basel Mission Home Board. The Mission school inspectors attempted to resolve school problems as they found them in the field, guided by the Missions' goal for education and what they considered good for the pupils and their parents. But because members of the Home Board were often unaware of the realities on the field, they did not usually appreciate the reform proposals. Some leading Missionaries did make attempts to provide education that would liberate the African, however.

Bohner and the BM Education Goal

Bohner, like most dedicated Missionaries of his time, fought against what the Europeans considered to be inhibiting factors to African development. He believed that polygamy, bride-price and slavery could be stopped through education. For him laziness was the root cause of all the vices and could only be eliminated when the virtue of work was taught at school. Hard work was considered by Bohner and people like him as the true test of Christian character. He further proposed Government subventions to Mission schools based on results and good functioning. The Government's reaction to their moves seems to have been one of indifference until 1907, when the first ever conference on education took place. However, the indifference gave scope to the Missions to operate schools to suit their purposes and convenience, the confusion of aims and curricula being made worse by the administrative system of Basel Mission education.

BM Administrative Weaknesses

Until 1897, each Missionary developed his own school system in his parish the way he thought fit, while the Home Board insisted on a central control. At the same time, there were frequent changes of personnel. Curriculum and syllabuses were different or shifted in respective stations and even within schools of the same parish. Schuler, who was a Basel Mission superintendent, argued that a common curriculum could solve the problems and, ostensibly in recognition of his arguments, he was appointed the first Inspector of Basel Mission schools in Cameroon, serving in that capacity from 1897 to 1903.

Reform Attempts under Schuler

Although Schuler had abandoned education after primary education, his training at the Seminary had equipped him for the challenges of the Mission field. He was an organised and pragmatic Missionary who in earlier service in Cameroon (1893-1895) had gathered useful experiences from the revolt of Cameroonians against German rule.

Poor health and the death of his wife had caused him to return to Germany in 1895 but his involvement in the translation of the Bible into Douala urged him to come back to Cameroon in 1897, this time as Inspector of schools. From 1901 to 1903 he was the superintendent of the Basel Mission. He extended the Mission field into the hinterlands by opening the Bali station in 1903. This was a significant development as it extended the Basel Mission educational activities to the thickly populated population of the Western Grassfields in the northwestern and western areas of the territory.

Schuler's greatest desire as inspector of schools was to expand and raise the standard of Basel Mission education. He introduced reforms to stop the practice of Missionary teachers passing on much of the teaching load to their untrained and unqualified Cameroonian colleagues, and limited the practice of giving educational responsibilities to Missionary clerics and evangelical duties to the lay Missionary teachers. He stopped the random opening of schools. Unlike his predecessors, who waited for approval from the Home Board before enforcing changes, Schuler reformed the school curricula without the approval of the Home Board. His guiding principle was the needs and expectations of the pupils, their parents, and the prospects of employment. By 1903, he had produced a common curriculum for all village schools in which the levels of reading, writing, arithmetic and religious knowledge were improved.

The Basel Mission Home Board had recommended reforms of Middle Schools and Boys' Schools in 1896, addressing the need for general and Christian education to satisfy Church and Government employment needs. Judging that the two schooling systems could not be reformed together, Schuler proposed a three-year programme of between 26 and 30 hours of schooling per week in the Middle Schools with greater emphasis on religious instruction and the German language. All graduates of the Middle Schools were supposed to acquire a good understanding of the German language, partly because the colonial administration had started to insist on it. To this effect, pupils had to recite Christaller's reader followed by the readers in use in Württemburg schools.

Imperial German Education Reform

Further to Schuler's reforms, the imperial German Government control over all educational agencies in Cameroon was introduced from 1910 by an education decree resulting from the 1907 education conference.

Government emphasised the teaching of German and insisted that the entire school curriculum be taught in German. A Government curriculum was issued for use in all schools in 1911. Hand-outs were prepared for most subjects in place of textbooks. This marked the beginning of state control over education in Cameroon.

FIGURE 2.2. Rev. Schuler, Knighted by Fon Fonyonga II at the Palace Court

The history syllabus comprised the study of German history, although hand-outs on pre-colonial and colonial Cameroon and German Governors in Cameroon were added to the history of Germany. For the benefit of the Christian Missions, the teacher-catechist students were taught the history of evangelisation in Cameroon. In Geography, general studies on Cameroon and Africa were followed by a study of the world. Finally, more emphasis was placed on Europe, particularly, Germany. In Arithmetic, pupils began with a study of basic arithmetical operations, and then followed up with the study of fractions, decimals and the metric system.

The syllabuses were not supported by textbooks, other than

the hand-outs that sometimes accompanied them. At the same time there were no competent teachers to teach them as most of the Missionaries were not trained to teach. Missionary recruits were mostly villagers with elementary education. Many Missions found high school education too expensive and also not necessary for recruitment into the Mission field.

Yet, each Missionary was considered more competent than his Cameroonian counterpart teacher. By 1913, over 50% of Missionaries were involved in education. Entering the seminary for Missionary training had become the great opportunity for further education in Switzerland and Germany. Yet, careful examination shows that few educated people opted for the Mission field at the beginning and those who were willing were usually sent to Asia which was considered culturally more developed and lucrative than Africa. Thus knowledge acquired by Missionary graduates to pass on to their pupils in the Missionary field was very limited in content and quality. Missionary low academic attainment level might well explain the inability of the missionaries to appreciate African culture and their bias against almost everything African.

Training Reforms

The absence of adequate structures for pedagogic instructions and further training in teaching methods combined with the absence of teaching-learning materials to hinder the attainment of good standards. The poor output was observed in 1911 by Dinkelacker, then Inspector of schools. To him, most Missionaries neither knew the subjects they taught nor had any systematic approach to teaching. Any serious intention to teach Africans the ability to learn and understand required a better preparation of those who had to teach; after all, Western education was totally strange and hardly made relevant to the prevailing African education system whose practices were often referred to as paganism.

In 1911, the authorities of the Mission became more seriously determined to provide good and qualified teachers, a concern that had been shown before but which had often been overtaken by circumstances of the period. In 1888, for example, George Munz, the first Mission inspector, had considered it necessary to retrain the teachers that the Basel Mission took over from the Baptist Missionary Society. This initiative would have continued alongside the recruitment of new teachers in subsequent years, but the rapid expansion of schools because of rivalry with the other denominations halted the exercise. More attention was focused on creating more schools than on training teachers. When Schuler became inspector of schools, he too complained about the quality of teachers and associated their weaknesses with the rapid expansion of schools.

Yet, it is not obvious that the training of teachers alone could have solved the problem of poor standards for the teacher had the dual responsibility of teaching and evangelising. Besides his full daily school load, he was responsible for morning and evening prayers, Sunday services, Sunday school classes, and doctrine classes for catechumens. Considered an educated and enlightened person, he was the main interpreter of the official information in his community. All these activities required time and preparation. Thus he could not adequately prepare his lessons. As a result, both pressure of time and the absence of teaching/learning materials reduced learning to the rote method.

Training Centres

1. *Middle Schools*

Education in the Middle Schools offered opportunities for most teacher-Catechists to be better trained and be more qualified. But the heavy demand for teachers in schools hardly allowed the pupils to complete the three-year course. Most of them were withdrawn at the end of the first and second years. Those who completed three years often gained employment with the colonial administration or private companies where they were better paid than teachers in Mission schools.

2. Seminaries

The creation of a seminary in 1898 was perhaps the first and best solution to the training of teachers. It was started in Bonaberi before being transferred to Buea in 1899 as a three-year course after the Middle School. Here, the student acquired skills in writing, a good knowledge of the Bible and Douala literature, besides reading and writing competences in the German language. The curriculum also included some aspects of Church and world history and the other subjects offered in the Middle Schools. Understandably, however, more time was allocated for Religious Instruction. In the final year the students were involved in teaching practice in schools.

Yet, the seminary failed to offer satisfactory professional training for its Middle School programmes gave the learners more of a "general education" character than professional training, thus preparing the graduates better for other lucrative employment in the colonial administration and in the private business sector. It was not therefore surprising that the Inspector of the Basel Mission schools complained in 1906 about teacher training in the seminary. The Mission ceaselessly faced the departure of many of their graduate teachers from the seminary. Matters worsened when in 1907 the Mission was obliged to reduce the salaries of Middle School graduates from 360 to 240 marks. This caused the resignation of many Mission teachers who easily gained employment in the colonial administration and private sector enterprises.

Furthermore, when the colonial Government assumed more responsibilities over education in 1911 and offered Government teachers better salaries, free medical care, lodging and paid holidays, most of the remaining Mission teachers decided to quit and join the Government service. Low salaries in Mission schools were generally associated with the assumption that each parish lodged and fed its teachers. It was also expected that these teachers had their own farms from where they or their wives produced food.

Dinkelacker's Reform Attempts

An important attempt to improve upon the Basel Mission schooling standards was proposed in 1906 by Dinkelacker, the schools inspector. He attributed part of the weakness of the teacher-catechists to school age. Most of them qualified as teachers at the age of about 16 years. At such an early age they could not competently take responsibility of a parish and a school and they could not command authority in their respective communities. When the Inspector proposed an extension of the Seminary courses to four years the Home Board in Basel rejected his proposal on grounds of its additional cost.

In 1910, Dinkelacker once again, suggested a further reorganization of the Basel Mission schooling system in Cameroon. He projected a new curriculum for teacher training which could enhance the acquisition of teaching skills and deeper knowledge of the subjects they had to teach. He also proposed a categorization of students in the Middle Schools into three classes:

Mature and serious pupils who could continue into the Seminary; those who were too young and had to stay longer at school; and those who could not handle responsibilities. He also recommended that the Village Schools be transformed into Middle Schools.

Dinkelacker's proposed reforms aimed not only at improving the training of teachers but perhaps more importantly, at training capable Cameroonians for future responsibilities in the forthcoming local church. The envisaged future leaders included pastors, catechists and teachers. It became necessary, therefore, to diversify the programme of training at the seminary. He recommended the study of the Bible, dogma and ethics, symbolism, homily and catechism, pastoral theology and the history of the church, as well as teaching methods, arithmetic, music and the German language.

Such a programme could have produced well-educated teachers but the Basel Mission Home Board again halted it on grounds of its being too vast and expensive. The Home Board only approved the up-grading of one Village School to a Middle

School and asked for special classes for evangelists to be added to the Middle Schools in Bonaberi and Lobetal.

A final effort to achieve reforms was mounted at a general conference of the field Missionaries in Douala from 22 to 28 April 1912. This was the last and also the most important attempt by the field Missionaries to overhaul the Basel Mission education system under the German colonial regime. Dinkelacker reminded participants of the important role of Mission education in liberating the pupils from all pagan practices and in their conduct before God. He considered that the pattern of Basel Mission education then in practice was unsuitable for such purposes. For him, success in liberating the pupils from evil absolutely required spiritually inspired Missionary educators and teachers. Such people, in his view, were lacking in the ranks of the Missionaries. He suggested a change of attitude on the part of the Missionaries so as to improve their relations with their Cameroonian counterparts for the sake of the very God they were striving to serve. Implicit in his argument was the inevitable search for better methods of teaching because, according to him, schooling did not have to end only in converting pagans to Christianity but, more importantly, at implanting and spreading a Christian culture through the training of competent and conscientious local assistants. To Dinkelacker, these were the bases for which the Basel Mission educational system had to be established.

The conference supported the addition of evangelist classes to Mangamba and Buea Middle Schools and emphasized a practical approach. They further requested the upgrading of Sakbayeme and Nyasoso schools to Middle School levels; the transformation of the German Schools into Middle Schools and the establishment of many more of such schools. When these suggestions for reforms reached the Home Board, it failed to give full satisfaction. It rejected the request by the conference to maintain the Seminary and instead asked for its replacement by two schools for evangelists offering two-year courses. The evangelist school did not satisfy the wishes of the Field Missionaries who insisted on a Seminary to enable the trainees to stay longer and gain maturity and deeper understanding of the subjects. They also believed that a full seminary training of four years was more beneficial than the two-year evangelist training that the Home Board proposed. The Home Board also proposed just one Missionary to each of the two evangelists' schools. But the Field Missionaries considered the activities too demanding on such a Missionary who also had to do the administration, teach, attend to students' spiritual and academic needs as well as conduct parish duties.

It is therefore evident that Basel Mission education during the German rule very often suffered from disagreement between the Home Board and the field Missionaries based on financial considerations. The Field Missionaries lived the experiences and understood the problems in Cameroon. Their suggestions were based on the realities in Cameroon. At that rate, the Mission's initial desire to educate local elites to establish the church in Cameroon remained a wish. Nonetheless, by the end of the German rule, the educational system had taken a specific pattern and the Mission's concern was to improve on its quality.

CHAPTER THREE

BASEL MISSION EDUCATION AND THE GERMAN REGIME: COLLABORATION AND/OR CONFRONTATION

It has already been indicated that the German colonial regime encouraged the establishment of the Basel Mission in Cameroon. The imperial Government assisted the Mission to start its educational activities in Cameroon when the Chancellor offered 3,000 marks which was followed subsequently by other financial assistance in the form of grants in aid.

At the beginning, Governor Soden (Pioneer German Governor of Cameroon) hoped that Missionaries could be used as judges in courts to hear cases between the indigenous people and also between Europeans and Africans. He expected Missionaries to maintain peace between ethnic groups and also keep vital statistics and other records.

These indications of favours and supports may lead to the misconception that as a German Mission, the Basel Mission had a glorious period under the regime. On the contrary, one of the principal inhibitions to the rapid and smooth development of Basel Mission education in Cameroon was the colonial Government. The Government failed to respect the conditions that the Mission requested on accepting to replace the British Baptist Missionary Society. The Mission's relation with the Government became characterized by disagreements on Government economic and social policies, especially during the reign of Governor von Puttkamer from 1895 to 1907.

Exploitation

1. Land/Economic Exploitation

Annexation of land for economic exploitation especially by private firms caused revolts from many Cameroonians, particularly along the fertile crescent of the Cameroon mountain region. In June and October 1896, the Chancellor of the Reich issued orders relating to the expropriation of land which became Crown lands.

He ruled that land belonging neither to private persons nor community could be considered Crown Land. But the regime in Cameroon was bent on supporting German plantation owners and economic interests. This perpetrated the expropriation of land occupied by Cameroonians. The Basel Mission opted to protect the Cameroonians and protested against the land policy, thereby identifying itself as defender of the Cameroonian communities.

Their failure to mitigate the expropriation of the land for plantation enterprise also affected their relations with Christian Cameroonians who relied on the intervention of the Mission. This loss of confidence in turn affected their educational and evangelical works. The Mission's appeal to the Colonial Office in Berlin to protect the interest, particularly of the Bakweri people in their land, led to the establishment of the first Land Commission appointed in January 1902, consisting of a German trader, a German plantation owner, two Missionaries (one from the Basel Mission and one from the Roman Catholic Mission) and a Government official. Rev. Schuler, then the Basel Mission Inspector in Cameroon, represented his Mission.

The Basel Missionaries were not satisfied with the resolution of the Land Commission which created a reserved area for the displaced people, however; the plantation companies had insisted that the Commission should leave it to the discretion of the respective plantations to determine the amount of land to be reserved. The Basel Missionaries appealed to the Chancellor of the Reich in 1903 and a special deputy was sent to assess the needs of the Cameroonians. More land was secured for the people in Buea. The efforts of the Mission restored Bakweri people's confidence and many of their villages asked for Basel Mission schools.

The Douala people were dissatisfied with the Basel Mission, feeling that the Mission did not do enough to defend their interests before the Government. For them as for many other Africans, land was indispensable. By the act of occupation signed between the Douala chiefs and the Germans in 1884, the German government acquired no land. In fact, the government pledged itself to recognise the existing property rights of Cameroonians in their land. It was therefore presumed that land had to be acquired by purchase or by conquest as in 1885 when the Government forced the Douala people to cede land. Indisputably, the Germans needed land for administrative houses, factories, wharves, railway stations, public buildings and other purposes. But their approach towards securing the land greatly disrespected the Douala people. They ordered occupants out of the town to the outskirts and the Douala people expected the Basel Mission to protect them as vigorously as they had done for the Bakweri people. They failed to achieve the same success perhaps because in the Bakweri land, the Mission was also fighting to maintain Mission land that had been seized by plantation owners. This disappointment affected the school enrolments and evangelical activities of the Basel Mission and further explains the strained relationship between the Douala people and the Germans up to and including the First World War period.

2. *Labour Exploitation*

The Basel Mission also defended Cameroonians against the scandals of forced labour. The Government had, among other methods, adopted the practice of using soldiers to recruit Cameroonians from the hinterland to work in the plantations. The colonial regime had also induced chiefs to take part in compelling recruitment. This became a lucrative band wagon upon which others climbed. But the living conditions in the labour camps and the hot climate of the coastal areas affected especially most of those who came from the cold climate areas of the interior highlands. Many died and many never returned to their villages. The people in these villages began to look upon all Europeans, including Missionaries, as enemies determined to eliminate their population and destroy their villages. This too had a toll on church attendance and school enrolments in the Mission Schools.

The Cameroonians affected by this policy, and who were not able to distinguish between colonial administrators, Missionaries, planters and traders, tended to hate all Europeans, including their religions and education. As a result, Cameroonian relations with all the Europeans were strained. For this reason, the Basel Mission decided to fight against the labour recruitment policy to save some of their out-stations from closing down. Besides, their struggle equally fitted within the conditions they had made in their formal application to the Government in 1886, namely, to protect the indigenous people from European exploitation.

3. *Language Policy*

Another area of confrontation between the Basel Mission and the colonial regime and which pre-occupied the Mission was the language problem. The Mission had indicated in their formal application that their intention was to use Cameroon languages for educational and evangelical purposes. Although the Government gave approval, many controversies followed in the course of time. The regime's disagreement with the Douala people and after 1908, against their former favourites, the Bali, whose languages were used for school instructions, caused the Government to stop the use of these languages even in the Vernacular Schools. The disenchantment by which the colonial administration fell out with the Bali people in 1908 manifested itself when they insisted that the Bali people (*Balitruppe*) should return the guns they once gave them during their imperialist wars to establish in the Grassfield region. Failure to recover these guns added to a flourishing trade and friendly relations between the Bali people and the Douala people to give the Germans the impression that the popularity of these people could eventually lead to such a union that might overthrow them from the territory. The regime thus found it necessary to check the spread of their two languages in the entire colony. This became visible in the new school policy of April 1910 which stated that "in native schools no other language is to be tolerated as a medium of instruction and as a subject except German and the actual dialect which is spoken by the people".

Until 1910, all Vernacular Schools in the forest zone used the Douala language and those in the Grassfields used Mungaka for school instruction. To respect the new language policy and operate Vernacular Schools required turning the many Cameroonian languages into writing. The Mission could neither afford the money nor the personnel to cope with such a regulation. This affected the enthusiasm of the Missionary workers and their output in schools. As such, the Home Board of the Basel Mission appealed to the Colonial Office in 1913 to reconsider the language policy, but up to the onset of war in 1914, no solution had been found.

4. *Liquor, Arms Dependence and Self-Reliance*

The Basel Mission was also strongly opposed to widespread sale of liquor and arms. As early as 1887, they issued an order forbidding the importation of liquor into the region they had bought from the British Baptists in Victoria. They also erected a plant in 1903 for the manufacture of soda water and other non-alcoholic drinks to counter alcohol consumption among Cameroonians.

To develop some level of economic sustenance and reduce the excessive exploitation of Cameroonians by German companies, the Basel Mission Trading Company (*Basler Missionshandlungsgesellschaft*) started importing goods from Europe and selling at affordable prices to the people. By 1900, the company began exporting Cameroonian goods, thereby encouraging Cameroonians to become independent producers. These missionary protective measures were followed by the opening of a

Missionary bank in Douala where they paid four per cent interest on Cameroonian deposit accounts. These attempts aroused the jealousy of German firms operating in Cameroon who thereafter refused to offer further assistance to Mission Schools.

BM Education and Other Missionary Societies

Another significant problem faced by the Basel Mission was from the other religious groups, the most formidable being Islam. The entire northern region of Cameroon was left to the Muslims and all attempts by the Basel Mission to open schools there were refused by the colonial administration. However, the imperial administration also made efforts to check further expansion of Islam to the south by persuading the Basel Mission to establish in Bali and Bamum.

Meanwhile, the Basel Mission enjoyed good relations with the American Presbyterian Mission. But when the German language was declared compulsory in schools, they contemplated handing over their schools to the Basel Mission since they could not easily afford German speaking teachers.

On the other hand, the Basel Mission's attitude towards the Catholics was unenthusiastic because initially, they were made to understand that they (the Basel Mission) were brought to Cameroon in order to keep the Catholics away from the German colony. They thus protested against the establishment of the Catholics in 1890, expressing fears of Catholic intrusion into their work. When they could not stop the Catholics, they suggested their confinement to specific areas. Relations between the two Missions were characterised by jealousy and rivalry that inevitably affected educational development through the hasty opening of schools. Pupils and staff of these schools developed strained relations towards each other. One could not be an adherent of one Mission Society and attend school in the other Mission without changing religious and doctrinal adherence.

BM Educational Achievements under the German Administration

Despite the problems faced by the Basel Mission, it is evident that their attempts to open schools in villages and main stations helped to establish colonial rule, at the same time as introduce literacy and Christianity. By touring and organising the schools, the Missionaries peacefully gained the support of Cameroonians for the regime. The school acted as a nucleus, radiating into the neighbourhood, especially during week-end evangelisations, Christian feast days and important occasions declared by the Government.

Table 3.1. The Evolution of School Enrolment during German Annexation

Year	Total Enrolment	Year	Total Enrolment
1887	228	1901	3185
1888	223	1902	4073
1889	284	1903	5025
1890	342	1904	6352
1891	578	1905	7426
1892	1457	1906	8617
1893	1497	1907	9198
1894	1281	1908	10098
1895	1281	1909	10619
1896	2102	1910	11785
1897	3204	1911	13683
1898	3278	1912	17833
1899	3372	1913	22818
1900	3290		

Source: Compiled by author

As noticed in the above table, between 1888 and 1898, school enrolment figures stood at 3,278 pupils including 389 girls. Further expansion into the interior led to the establishment of 19 main stations located at Bagam, Bali, Bana, Banjoun, Bangwa, Besongabang, Bombe, Bonaberi, Bonaku, Buea, Edea, Foumban (Bamum), Lobetal, Mangamba, Ndogbea, Ndongue, Nyasoso, Sakbayeme and Victoria. By 1913, there were 384 elementary schools with 22,818 pupils under 409 teachers in all these stations. The evolution of school enrolment as detailed in table 1 was consistently on the increase, rising more than one-hundredfold from the 228 pupils when they took over the schools from the London Baptist Missionary Society in 1887 to 22,818 in 1913, i.e. in twenty-six years.

At the outbreak of the war, the Mission also had 16 Middle Schools, equivalent to secondary schools with 1,748 pupils. Two of the secondary schools in Douala supplied the administration and other employers with well-educated people, competent in the German language and culture. Still in Douala at Akwadorf town, they had two vocational/technical schools offering courses in carpentry, cabinet-making and mechanical engineering.

They also had a teacher training institution which by 1914 had 53 students. Thus, in spite of all the difficulties that the Mission encountered, they established an educational system within a Christian culture that even the First World War could not dismantle. Its success and acceptance was so deeply rooted that the Mission's activities could survive unaided during the non-Missionary period from 1914 to 1925.

The Basel Mission education under the Germans suffered tensions, contradictions and paradoxes generated by political, economic and social conflict of interests between the government and the missions. There were also disagreements of various degrees sometimes within individual parishes and sometimes between different parishes, but more often, between the Home Board and the Field Missionaries. These frictions produced inconsistencies that significantly affected the development of education. The contradictions combined with the catalogue of disagreements that the Mission had with the Government and other Missions to attenuate Basel Mission educational achievements. The education pattern developed by the Mission and the liberty that they enjoyed under the German regime influenced their activities under subsequent regimes and had a significant impact on those who took over the management of the schools.

The Basel Mission established an educational policy that was accepted as the official German colonial education policy in Cameroon up to the eve of the First World War. The policy of the Missions on the promotion of local languages was a huge achievement which, if supported by the Government, could have enhanced better educational attainment and fostered creative thinking because the pupils and their African teachers would have been working and thinking in a language that reflected their culture and environment.

Table 3.2. Schools and enrolments by 1912

Proprietors	No. of schools	Enrolment
American Presbyterian Mission	97	6,545
Basel Mission	319	17,833
Pallotine Catholic Mission	151	12,532
German Baptist Mission	57	3,151
Government Schools	4	833
Total	628	40,894

Source: Kaiserlichen StatistischenAmte; Statstisches Jahrbuch fur das Deutsche Reich 1910-1931

In addition, the Basel Mission education policies enabled Cameroonians to be protected from the excesses of German colonial socio-economic and political exploitations. The Mission, for this reason, may be exonerated from the usual charge of Government-Mission conspiracy in exploitation, and be commended for educational achievements. However, the expulsion of the

German colonial regime from Cameroon in 1916, following their defeat in the First World War, thwarted further developments in educational activities. Educational developments during the German colonial administration were therefore dominated by the Basel Mission as demonstrated in the table above.

CHAPTER FOUR

CAMEROONIAN RESPONSES TO BASEL MISSION EDUCATION UNDER THE GERMAN REGIME

Apparently, education, more than any other imperialistic factor, facilitated the German annexation of Cameroon. The introduction of Missionary education in 1844 had encouraged the coastal elites of Cameroon to request for the support of Queen Victoria's assistance in the expansion of English culture in the territory and Cameroonians believed that education was the "magic" formula to European culture and advancement. This African discernment of the values of Western education and consequent positive reaction motivated by expectations of economic, social, political and cultural developments preceded colonialism.

Cameroonian reactions often conflicted with imperialistic impulses. But it would be an exaggeration to argue that, throughout the three decades of German rule, the responses were always confrontational. German rule points to three possible periods that characterize Cameroonian reactions and participation in the development of Western education. The first period logically preceded the beginning of pacification wars and oppressive German rule in different parts of the territory. During this period there were still high expectations from both sides, a considerable degree of collaboration and mutual respect of both parties. Nachtigal, the chief negotiator for German annexation, pointed out in his report of August 1884 that Cameroonians asked for education and were even ready to pay for its establishment and development.

Thus, on the part of Cameroonians, there was enthusiasm and determination for the establishment of German education. King Bell's family helped the first German appointed teacher, Theodore Christaller, to study the Douala language and to produce learning and teaching materials. The Bell family also provided land for the first school in Douala.

Similar excitement and attitudes were expressed by other Cameroonian leaders as the Germans advanced further inland. When the first German party arrived in the Western High Plateau of what is described variously as "Grassfields", "Bamenda Highlands" or "Bamenda Province", they were requested by the paramount ruler of Bali, Fon Galega I to introduce their system of education in the area. Chilver argues that the people of this area and especially from Bali wanted to learn and understand what made the "white man" different from the African. Lekunze confirms that most Cameroonians were so impressed by the first German visitors that they tended to accept anything European uncritically and with fervour. The positive impressions created by the team leader, Zintgraff, the first European visitor to Bali kingdom, motivated the ruler, Fon Galega I to invite Missionaries to his territory. When the Mission delayed to respond to the invitation, he petitioned in 1897 to the Colonial Office in Berlin requesting specifically, for the services of the Basel Mission to establish a school. In 1900, his son and successor to the throne, Fon Fonyonga II renewed the request.

The Germans might have misconstrued the persistent appeals for a desire to establish the Christian church, but Fon Galega's shrewdness in handling issues on religion tends to dismiss that argument. Galega avoided talking much on religious matters and was ready to receive many European religious denominations provided they brought education and change to his people.

This is perhaps one luminous illustration that Africans knew what they wanted out of European imperialism right from their first contact. By dismissing Zintgraff's question on religion as "futility of brain racking for things not seen" and preferring to receive more than one denomination "since good things must be taken from all sides", Galega clearly exemplified African contemporary expectation of imperialism. It can therefore be argued that African rulers were not stupid in submitting their autonomy to Basel Mission Europeans.

FIGURE 4.1. Basel Mission House Bali

Further evidence to illustrate the desire for education rather than religion can be discerned from the experiences of F. Ernst, the first Missionary to arrive in the Grassfields. On Ernst's arrival in Bali in 1903, Fon Fonyonga II and his people constructed a residence for the Missionary and a school. They were very hospitable to the Missionaries. Even before Missionary Ernst fully settled, the Fon had submitted himself to be taught how to read and write German.

It is important to note that the Missionaries were as interested in learning the African language and way of life as the Africans were of learning theirs. There was thus some level of equality and mutual respect, unlike the approach of the imperial administration that saw Africans as second-grade human beings.

Furthermore, the Fon supported the education of his people by participating in the recruitment of pupils and with a donation of 200 marks for the purchase of slates.

FIGURE 4.2. B M School Bali (first school in the Grassfields): staff, pupils and the Fon at the front rank 1905

He personally supervised school attendance and punished when necessary. His interest and participation led to the rapid growth of the school which is said to have registered 450 pupils including 30 girls by 1905. His own children were in this pioneer batch including Tita Sosiga who later went to Germany for further studies.

The Fons' interest and participation also demonstrate African effort in spreading and promoting education, which literature on African education has tended to ignore. Graduates of this school included the son of king Njoya of Bamum and Lima of Bali, who became a popular teacher and helped in opening other schools during the German and early British rule, as well as Abraham Ngankou of Bansoa who became the first Bamileke pastor.

Similar to the Bali experience was that of Njoya of Bamum who did not hesitate to learn how to read and write. He helped in building the school structure and enrolling pupils in the first school opened in Foumban in 1906. Njoya's interest in European education was so overwhelming that he gave up Islam to become a Christian but was refused baptism because he was a polygamist (Lekunze E.F;1987).

Because German colonialists and Missionaries tended to marginalise these rulers, their interests in European education declined. For instance, a disagreement between Fon Fonyonga II and the Germans over the failure to retrieve 2,000 German guns from the kingdom affected their relations and in turn led to the decline of education. Secondly, because the rulers could not bear to see their children being flogged at school, pupils enrolled during the later years were rarely from the royal or noble families. Finally, none of them was ready to renounce polygamy for the sake of baptism. Therefore Cameroonian attitudes towards the introduction of western education were initially enthusiastic but the sustenance of that excitement and continued hospitality to colonial and Missionary educators depended largely on the responses of Europeans to Cameroonian interests. When colonialism was repressive and disrespectful to traditional culture, Cameroonians became apprehensive and resentful.

The second phase of Cameroonian reaction to education under German rule can be situated during Governor Jesco Von Puttkamer's unpopular reign[21] from 1895 to 1906. His brutality, extensive child labour practices and perpetration of immorality among his raiding conscripts led to a general resistance in most parts of the territory, seriously affecting school attendance. He got dishonourable recall but while his exploitative tenure lasted, sending children to school was seen as exposing them for recruitment into forced labour in German plantations, railway and road construction.

---

21 Cf. Stoecker H.

FIGURE 4.3. Governor Jesco Von Puttkamer (1895 – 1906)

In Douala, (German) attempts to move Cameroonians from their old plateau residence at Jos Town to the outskirts of the town in order to expropriate the beautiful site for exclusive European residence met with strong resistance. The expropriation decision added to the violation of the promise made during the discussion preceding the treaty of annexation. The Germans promised to maintain the Douala peoples' intermediary role in trade but tactfully failed to include that clause in the annexation treaty. The failure to fulfil these promises further aggravated the deteriorating relations.

The Basel Mission's original intentions were to evangelise and to educate Cameroonians, and these objectives were warmly welcomed in Cameroon, particularly because of the educational dimension. The rapid expansion of the Mission beyond the coastal areas was because of the people's demand for the establishment of schools. For example, Fon Galega I of Bali applied through Zintgraff, the first European to arrive in the savanna belt of Cameroon in 1889, for a Mission educational establishment so that his people might gain from European education.

In 1897, the Fon appealed to the Colonial authorities for the Basel Mission to establish in Bali and after his death in 1900, his successor, Fonyonga II made several reminders for the Mission to establish in Bali. From 1903, when the Mission arrived in Bali, it became clear that the desire for Western knowledge was the underlying reason for their invitation. The Fon demonstrated his desire for education through the hospitality he offered the Missionaries and the rapidity with which he had the school built and gathered pupils to start learning. He made the Rev. Ernst, who was the head of the Mission, formerly of Lobetal, his personal adviser – *Nkom* of the Fon.

It is possible to see the Fon's intention to attract education to be distinguished from a desire to have access to Christian religion. His father, Fon Galega had dismissed any discussions on religion with Zintgraff, philosophising that religion was a matter that could neither be seen nor heard and that he welcomed all religious denominations.

The Fon supervised regular attendance at the school and requested all sub-chiefs within his kingdom to send children to the school. By 1905, the school had three classes. Unprecedentedly, the Fon declared Sunday a day of rest throughout his kingdom. In 1907, a teacher-catechists school was opened for the region which began with 130 students recruited from the graduates of the school. To further illustrate the people's desire for education, in March 1907, the Fon and his people selected 283 pupils for the school but the Mission could only find room for 160.

It is interesting to note that of all the graduates leaving the school, only 150 had been baptised before the end of German rule. Evidently, widespread interest was for Western education and not for the Christian religion, perhaps because of its preaching against such customs as polygamy, traditional sacrifices and ancestral veneration. Cameroonian interests in the Mission were therefore, for pragmatic reasons and utilitarian purposes. The welcome given the Missionaries and their school system was because of the Cameroonian desire to be prepared for the new system of Governance and particularly to benefit from opportunities emerging from the new economy. However, the interest was often wider than that. Chilver told the author of interviews she conducted with elderly men in 1960. The men said they had hoped to "capture" the knowledge of the Germans through Western education and make it their own. Many said they later regretted that they had been unwilling to submit to the Basel Mission's continuous discipline of schooling.

As in Bali, the Basel Mission was warmly welcomed by Njoya, king of the Bamum. The king quickly became so friendly with Göhring, leader of the Mission, that he renounced Islam with the intention of becoming a Christian. The mosque in the palace was replaced by a church. The first school was started in 1906 with 60 boys and 51 girls. Njoya and his people were disappointed when the Missionaries could not recruit more than this number. Of the first 52 baptised people, 28 were wives and daughters of the king. This explains the predominance of the protestant faith in the Bamum land and especially in Foumban.

Meanwhile, the Missionaries refused baptizing the king and his nobles, despite their regular attendance at catechumen classes and church services. The fact that the Missionaries insisted on monogamy as a precondition for baptism, marked a decline in Christianity and Missionary education in Bamum, even though the Mission school had an enrolment of 600 pupils and five Basel Missionaries in 1914.

King Njoya and his people realized that the Christian culture was opposed to their own pattern of life and that European education was the most suitable means to orientate people to the new pattern of life. The king therefore opened his own school and revived his own personal scripts which he had earlier invented. He transformed the writing from idiographic to syllabic symbols

- of a set of codes, and also invented a secret language. This school became popular and retained the Bamum palace culture.

These cross-cultural confrontations were noticeable almost everywhere the Mission established in Cameroon. Lekunze has argued that the cultural confrontation underlay the slow development of education and Christianity in Cameroon. This opinion echoes Hallden's remark that Basel Mission failures resulted from lack of acquaintance with, and dismissal of, the people's culture. Jonas Dah equally condemns the Mission's unscrupulous approach at fighting heathenism without regard for the peoples' culture. He holds that this factor militated against the acceptance of the religion.

Yet, as a member of the Conference of Protestant Missionary Society, which since 1866 had stressed cultural relativism and opposed the Hanseatic traders' laissez-faire attitude while condemning the national chauvinism of most colonial enthusiasts, the Basel Mission was expected to display a more humane attitude and cultural tolerance towards Cameroonians.

This cultural weakness of the Mission may be attributed to their pietistic background which led them to treat strange cultures in the spirit of religious rigour and confuse Christian education with Europeanization. It may also be attributed to a feeling of cultural superiority and national pride as it was the case with most people of the Aryan race of the period.

Yet, Gustave Warneck observed that German Missionary efforts, unlike the English, had more capacity and will to accommodate themselves to foreign peculiarities. Ingrained therefore in the spirit of pietism, which implied a rigorous distinction of those who were saved by maintaining a higher standard of ethical behaviour from those who were not, the Missionaries expected their converts to abandon their cultures and practice the ethics brought by Christian education. This narrow perception of Africans seriously affected Basel Mission education. The Missionaries never contested African intellectual competence but felt that African culture inhibited their development. Thus, the conversion process demanded a rejection of traditional customs and values. In other words, a polygamous Christian convert had to reject all but one wife.

The Missionaries never cared about what happened to the rejected women. According to Rudin, the Basel Mission sometimes allowed their Christians to keep all their wives but there is no indication in the literature consulted so far to confirm that the Mission agreed to baptise any polygamists. Pastor Vohringer applied in 1911 for permission to baptise a polygamist and had the support of Dinkelacker, the Mission school inspector and Lutz the Field chairman, but no positive response was received from the Home Board. Lekunze asserts that the anti-polygamist attitude of the Mission explains the slow and limited expansion of their Mission Field coverage in Cameroon.

The Christian ethical rigidity, together with the inculcation of disrespect for certain aspects of indigenous cultures, created tension between the Mission-educated people and the traditional authorities. The society regarded the educated people as subversive of the traditional rules and regulations. The tension was heightened by the abrupt departure of the Missionaries when the First World War started. This seriously affected schooling during the non-Missionary period.

It should also be observed that the determination of the Missions to see schooling as the means of evangelisation was reiterated by Raaflaub, when he made it clear that whoever went to school was expected to become a Christian. Indeed, all school graduates were baptized even when they were not committed. However, it was also negative because the Missionaries failed to see the desire of Africans for education. Most Africans received baptism without conviction but simply in order to have their education and attain personal goals. It was held that with education it was easy to have money, have a job, acquire European goods and improve one's social status. For this reason, those who got educated and baptized were not necessarily committed Christians and could not therefore sustain the Christian ideals that the Missionaries fought to establish.

CHAPTER FIVE

BASEL MISSION EDUCATION UNDER BRITISH AND POSTCOLONIAL REGIMES: 1916-1966

The First World War brought an end to German patronage of the Basel Mission in Cameroon and ushered in an era of uncertainties characterized by the apprehensions of the new regimes – British and French. The initial expulsion of all German nationals, including Missionaries, and the delay in bringing back the Missions greatly hampered the work they had started under the Germans. The hostilities exhibited against the Basel Mission by the British and even worse, by the French significantly affected their educational contributions. The combined impact of the various political, social and economic problems of the period on Basel Mission education should be seen as part of the package in their contributions to educational development at the end of their work in 1966. The Basel Mission had to manage new relationships with the new colonial ruling regime, with the Cameroonians and other contemporary Missionary societies. These inter-relationships impacted on Basel Mission education.

The decade following the beginning of the First World War may be termed the Non-Missionary years. This period has been described as the "dark days" by Solomon Shu and as the "priestless years" by Anthony Ndi. It was a calamitous time for Christian Missionary work in Cameroon. The total expulsion of all German Missionaries of all denominations from Cameroon and the delay in replacing these Missionaries particularly in the British occupied zone, almost ruined the decades of educational efforts which the Basel Mission had exerted.

In the French zone, the Basel Mission was totally excluded and replaced by a French Protestant Mission (*Societé des Missions Évangeliques de Paris*). All Basel Mission stations and schools in the area were taken over by that French Protestant Mission. Compounded by the economic crisis of the 1930s and the effects of the Second World War, these ructions dampened missionary spirits towards investment in schools. Furthermore, the Roman Catholic Mission quickly re-established in the British zone as permission was granted to the Mill Hill Fathers in 1922. The Mill Hill Fathers had British connections and were therefore seen to be favoured by the new colonial government. The eventual greater development and expansion of the Roman Catholic Mission vis-à-vis the Basel Mission during the British period (1916-1961) evolved from these developments.

WWI and the Non-Missionary Period – 1914-1925

The First World War fought between Germany and the Allied Powers started in Cameroon on 3rd August 1914. By December of that year, practically all of Southern Region of Cameroon had been captured by the Allied forces. However, Germany resisted in the north until 19 February 1916 when she capitulated.

During the war, civil life was replaced by disarray as Cameroonians were divided by allegiance to the two opposing camps. In the confusion, looting, vandalism and all sorts of atrocities were widespread. Education stopped and school buildings became military barracks. Over 21,000 Cameroonians who were German supporters, comprising Christians, church workers (including teachers) followed their German friends and took refuge on the island of Fernando Po. The departure of these Missionaries and their Cameroonian followers crippled further developments in Mission education during the decade after 1914.

Following the early period of the war when the southern part of Cameroon was conquered, a joint Anglo-French administration under General Dobell attempted, through a condominium, to re-instate normal life from December 1914. But fundamental differences in British and French colonial policies and attitudes inhibited any chances of success. In March 1916, following the complete defeat of the Germans, the two powers did not hesitate to partition Cameroon for their respective rules. The British took just one fifth of the territory, the part that stretched on the borders of their Nigerian colony, from Lake Chad to the Atlantic Ocean. The French took the rest of the territory, including the Douala basin for which they seriously negotiated in order to have access to the sea for the French Equatorial Africa.

The French were quick to replace the German Missionaries in their own zone of influence. In January 1920, the Basel Mission Home Board reluctantly handed over their assets in that zone to the French protestant Mission, *Societé des Missions Évangeliques de Paris* which was succeeded in 1957 by *Églises Évangeliques du Cameroun (EEC)*.

On the British side, it was a lengthy and fruitless process of negotiation with British Missionary Societies to replace German Missionaries in their own zone. Not until 1922 did the first Missionary Society, the Roman Catholic Mill Hill Fathers, accept to replace the Pallotine Fathers in the English zone. On the Basel Mission side, there was a long drag. But, thanks to pressures from the Protestant International Missionary Organisations and the active role played by Swiss Missionaries (who presented Basel Mission as a Swiss and not a German Mission), coupled with other circumstances arising from the international scene, the Basel Mission was at last allowed to resume activities in Cameroon in 1925.

Rev. Allegret, head of the French Protestant Mission, played a major role in discouraging the British Protestant Missions from replacing the Basel Mission in the British Cameroons. He wanted to extend the influence of the Paris Evangelical Mission that was already established in the French sphere to the British zone.

Those were days of instability. Yet, the absence of the European Missionaries did not stop all Mission schooling in the British zone. When the war ceased in Cameroon in 1916, some enthusiastic Cameroonians attempted to revive education. The number of schools and statistics of the pupils are unknown because there were no records and no central organisation. The quality of education was inevitably perfunctory, since most of the teachers were unqualified, many of the good ones having fled with the Missionaries to Equatorial Guinea. The curricula were determined by the teachers and taught either in the local language or in German, a thing intolerable to the new colonizers. Pastor Johannes Litumbe Ekeze, who became the first Cameroonian pastor in the British territory, supervised the Mission activities alongside the French Protestant Missionaries from the French zone. People like Francis Lima of Bali who served as a Basel Mission teacher before the war in the Bamileke country and all over the Bamenda Grassland opened schools and bought German-English dictionaries from which they learnt and taught the pupils.

Besides, there were financial difficulties to contend with. For, while the French Protestant Mission supported a few, most schools depended on voluntary contributions. School attendance generally, therefore, depended on the social and financial abilities of the pupils. It was only to be understood that in the planting seasons, most of the schools were closed. The British Mandatory Government, on assumption of the administration of the territory, referred to this type of school as "Hedge schools" or "Bush schools". So deplorable was the situation that the only organised school is said to have been the Basel Mission School at Tiko which was supervised directly by the French Evangelical Mission in Douala.

Added to the hazards was the inability of the teachers to collaborate with local traditional authorities. Education and evangelisation in most communities were considered subversive to traditional order and therefore became anathema to the local traditional authorities. Whereas Missionaries had recognised the necessity to cloak the subversive tendencies of Christian education, through some respect to the local traditions, the Cameroonian teachers openly opposed local traditions, deeming them contradictory to the Christian doctrine.

A curious phenomenon in these times too was the

sociopolitical impact (emerging from the Basel Mission schooling system during the non-Missionary period) linked to the concept of "Ethiopianism". This phenomenon was identified with African nationalism expressed through the medium of the church. It was derived from Psalm 68:31 which states that "Ethiopia shall stretch forth her hands to God". Whereas the episode in South and East Africa, where the phenomenon was first noticed, could be attributed to racial discrimination arising out of the colour-bar policy of the white settler (since racial policies led to "separatist" churches that became anti-government movements), that of Cameroon was derived from increasing signs of superstitions. A form of syncretic doctrine, expressed in practices of mixed Christianity and superstition, was emerging among the followers of the Basel Mission. Traditional rulers dreaded this form of the Christian religion because of its eventual competition with local forms of belief. This led the colonial administrators to draw the conclusion that the problems could eventually develop into seditious ethiopianism as in South Africa and Nyasaland.

The particular case in Cameroon referred to the Makaya episode. Makaya, whose actual names were Monica Abandeng, was a catechumen of the Basel Mission in Mamfe who claimed to have seen a vision where God promised her the supply of enough food to feed the people (see Ruxton in NAB. Ba1921). She then asked all her followers to take an oath to resist all authorities and not to work. This was a potential social hazard, which if disseminated through the school system, could be socio-politically disastrous. This particular problem was one of the major factors that moved the Government to reconsider the return of the Basel Mission.

Britain had ruled successfully in India and the Gold Coast in close collaboration with the Basel Mission and the failure to find a suitable British Missionary Society to replace the Mission in Cameroon could therefore not pose any major threat to the British Government. After all, the British protestant Missions were hesitant to supplant the Basel Mission, since they all belonged to the International Conference of Mission Societies (ICMS), whose solidarity was at its peak during this period. The Lake Mohonk

Conference of the International Council of Missions on 1 October 1921 and the Inter-Denominational Missionary Conference of 23 November 1921 helped the Basel Mission to regain their stations in Cameroon. For on each occasion, the Basel Mission representative presented the urgent need for their presence in Cameroon. These contacts eventually impacted on the entire International Council of Protestant Missions. J. H. Oldham, the General Secretary of the Council (who happened to be an English man) took responsibility with the British Government to allow the Basel Mission to return to Cameroon. The Government too was concerned about the reports of the colonial administrators. Above all, however, it was the visiting Missions, such as the Phelps-Stokes Commission, that contributed to the return of the Basel Mission in 1925. The Fund was founded by Caroline Phelps-Stokes for research on Black American education. The American Baptist Foreign Missionary Society had requested the Phelps-Stokes Fund to sponsor research on African education so as to make proposals for an education policy, especially on social, hygienic, religious and economic matters. The Fund urged all agencies providing education to participate in the development and implementation of the policy for education (M. B. Gwanfogbe; 2006:117- 118). This somehow hastened the return of the Basel Mission to resume educational activities in Cameroon.

The Mandate

On several counts, the second part of Basel Mission work in Cameroon (after WWI) was very unlike the first part (1886-1914). The Mission was limited only to British Southern Cameroons, their establishments in the French mandated area having been taken over by French protestant missionaries. The Basel Mission had to operate under the British mandated administration thereafter and no longer under the German colonial administration. This implied a new language for education, new colonial culture and a new pattern of loyalty. Attempts to solve the language problem through the use of the local languages they had earlier developed did not take long to encounter difficulties.

These differences were compounded by the enormous challenges encountered by the Basel Mission to regain admission into Cameroon after WWI. Added to this, the structural organisation started under the Germans had also been disrupted during the non-Missionary period (1914-1925). Thus this period was characterized by a drag and negative turnaround for the Basel Mission educational achievements.

However, Basel Mission activities did survive, thanks to the zeal and devotion of some Cameroonian evangelists and Christians. The supervision of Pastors Ekeze and Modi Din of the Paris Evangelical Mission in Douala, in particular, was very significant. For, during the German period, these pastors belonged to the Basel Mission but became absorbed by the French Mission at the defeat of the Germans in Cameroon during the war. Their occasional evangelical visits inspired the Christians in the British-occupied zone to maintain their faith and to continue with their school efforts. By the time the Missionaries returned in 1925, six main stations with schools had survived in Bali, Besongabang, Bombe, Buea, Nyasoso and Victoria. These schools were not adaptable to British colonial school regulations because the teachers, who had been German trained, taught in either Douala or Mungaka languages; they could not use British teaching materials. Meanwhile, the Basel Mission School at Tiko had enjoyed special attention from the pastors coming from Douala. It was better organized when compared to the other surviving schools.

In 1926 when the new Nigerian Ordinance on education was adopted in the territory, these teachers were invariably disadvantaged, their knowledge of German no longer being useful. They had to learn English in order to continue as teachers.

After World War I

Generally, post WWI Basel Mission education offered only elementary (primary) education, subdivided into Vernacular and English schools. As explained earlier, Vernacular schools were located in villages and instructions were either in Douala schools in the Forest zone (currently South West Region) or Mungaka for those in the Grassfield area (current North West Region).

Before the colonial education code was introduced, vernacular schools ran for first three years. The colonial education code brought it down to two years and graduates continued in the English school at the Infants Two level. The brilliant graduates, however, were admitted into Standard One, which was the third level of the English school. Graduates of the Vernacular school could read and write in the local language but not in English. Those who did not continue to the English school became teachers and Evangelists for the Mission.

The English school was patterned on the Colonial Education code in which the pupil started in Infants One and did two years to complete the Infants level. The next level was the junior primary which started from Standard One and ran up to Standard Four. Some people left school at this level and were employed. It was expected that at this stage the pupil would have acquired all the reading, speaking and writing skills necessary for adequate self-expression in any function.

Those who moved up to senior primary had to do two years to obtain the school certificate upon success in the promotion examinations at the end of Standard Five to move to Standard Six. The certificate Examination was initially set from Lagos and later from Enugu and when Southern Cameroons had a Regional status in 1954, the examination was set from Buea. The Basel Mission had very few schools in the 1920s that offered education up to standard six because this required more qualified English-speaking teachers than they could afford.

The Nigerian Education Code used in British Cameroons apparently encouraged close collaboration between the government and Missions, but imposed restraints on the Mission when compared with their situation under the Germans. The Basel Mission authorities no longer enjoyed the liberty they had under the Germans since the government required the Missions to conform to the new regulations before receiving government assistance. There was no alternative here since the desire of parents was for their children to have such education as could gain them employment under the new regime. The anti-Christian reactions of some parents during the non-missionary period had reinforced dislike for Mission education, which most parents considered a disguise for the propagation of Christianity. Since the Mission rarely posted qualified teachers to villages that were unenthusiastic about the Christian religion, most Cameroonians concluded that Mission education aimed essentially at evangelising.

Another range of problems faced by the Basel Mission in education at this early stage of the British rule could be attributed to the continued disagreements between the Field Missionaries and the Home Board. The Home Board met in 1927 to re-organize schools in Cameroon, and as in the German period, their emphasis was on the evangelical work of schools. To achieve this aim, the Board resolved to operate fewer schools to which Missionaries could be posted to ensure an effective implantation of Christianity through high quality education. It was believed that good education would attract many pupils. Thus the policy of *Drang nach Schulbildung* (educational zeal) was adopted to guide future educational development in Cameroon. This policy ignored the importance the Mission had earlier given to mass evangelisation through schooling; it ignored the impact of inter-denominational competition on the school system. These omissions rendered field practice burdensome. But practitioners in the field remained focused on winning large numbers of converts using varied methods.

It was difficult to stop the "Hedge Schools" or "Bush Schools" opened in the absence of the Missionaries. The Mission could not refuse applications for teachers from Christians who had opened schools on behalf of the Mission in their villages either; such refusals would be considered anti-evangelical. Yet the Mission lacked qualified teachers for all these schools, the majority of the teachers being untrained and some having only had the four-year Village School education. They could barely give initiation to the **3Rs** – **R**eading, **W**riting and **A**rithmetic, with some emphasis on a fourth **R** of religious instruction. Some of the schools also had very few pupils, whereas the operation of schools with such few numbers on religious basis contradicted the education code and brought conflict with the Government.

The administration asked for the closure of such schools which were over 300 in number by 1927. After several appeals to the colonial headquarters in Lagos, the Mission was allowed to operate them as religious schools on condition that neither English nor Arithmetic were taught there. Only reading, writing and religious instruction were taught in the vernacular, to enable pupils to read the Bible. However, the regulation also gave room for Government recognition of religious schools with more than 10 registered pupils. Based on this regulation, H. Wildi, the supervisor of Basel Mission Schools, applied for the registration of all the schools as a mark of the Mission's collaboration with the government. They became known as Infant Vernacular Schools. As such, the Home Board's objective of a few schools and the British colonial regime's desire for all schools to conform to the ordinance were not respected. The reality was determined by events in the Mission Field.

Schools that conformed to the regulations, gained government financial assistance and became known as Assisted Schools. These were elementary schools using English as a medium of instruction. Pupils admitted to these schools were graduates of the Infant Vernacular Schools. These assisted Schools provided a four-year course leading to a standard four certificate. English, arithmetic, writing and religious knowledge were the principal subjects on the curriculum. Those who continued after this level could do two more years to obtain standard six certificates in a full primary school.

To be recognised and to obtain government assistance, a school had to have a qualified teacher. The idea of certificated or qualified teachers posed a major problem to the Mission. For a solution, they first asked for the assistance of the Government to select some of the former German-trained teachers for in-service training under Government officials. They could thereby acquire

English Language and improve on their teaching skills. They also imported trained teachers from Nigeria and the Gold Coast but these teachers were similarly handicapped, not being able to teach religious instruction and hygiene, which were taught in local languages.

Oettli, the Basel Mission Inspector, negotiated with British authorities in 1927 for Missionary teachers to be awarded "Honorary Certificates" on passing the Junior Cambridge Examination. Finally, the Government also allowed the Mission to send pupil teachers for training at the Government Teachers Training College in Buea, initially known as Normal School. The first Basel Mission student-teacher was admitted into the Normal School in 1931, but by1937 the number had increased to seven and by 1944 there were 13 in the school. These various measures enabled the Mission to open three new primary schools in Bali, Besongabang and Buea headed by the Missionaries, Hummel, Heiser and Grest respectively.

Another one started at Nyasoso under Ulmann and in 1932, they opened a school in Weh alongside a Mission Station headed by Wilhein Schneider.

Another aspect of government regulations that affected the Basel Mission education concerned the structure of classes. All post-infant classes had to study History, Geography, Nature Study and Hygiene in English but Mission infant schools had no introduction to English language studies. At first, they solved the problem by extending their infant classes to the third year during which English language was introduced. But this lengthened the duration of schooling and increased the expenditure on the Mission's budget. Besides, it was against the government regulation of two years for that level. It was therefore soon abandoned and English was introduced in the second year.

Since government grants depended on the quality of teachers and the application of government regulations and because the world economic depression also affected the Mission, all efforts were made to abide by the rules. Thus from 1931, the Mission was able to receive the first grant of £50 and by 1932, six of their schools qualified for grants. The increased number can also be explained by the change in the policy for award of grants.

FIGURE 5.1. Basel Mission School Besongabang

In 1932, the Board of Education decided to shift the condition from achievements of individual schools to block grants to each category of schools under each Mission. All Elementary Schools (Standard I-IV) received £100 and all Primary or Middle Schools (Standard V-VI) received £150, while Boarding Schools for girls received £200. Government subvention was therefore a motivation for closer collaboration between Missions and the administration and gave opportunity for the government to control Mission schools. At the same time, Mission competition for government subvention led to greater respect of government regulations and an improvement of the quality of education.

The world economic depression had a significant impact on education in general, but particularly on Mission education. The fall in prices of Cameroon products and the closure of business companies reduced employment possibilities. The fall in income also reduced Government finances and cut down on employment. This discouraged the parents who were already unable to pay for schooling, their income having significantly dropped. School enrolment in consequence also significantly dropped from 1931 to 1933 as shown on Table 5.1.

Table 5.1. BM Schools Enrolments during the Mandate Period

Year	Boys	Girls	Total	Assisted Schools	Unassisted Schools
1925	2,920	287	3,207	1	113
1926	3,458	477	3,935	1	129
1927	7,155	-	-	1	305
1928	5,518	549	6,067	-	255
1929	5,120	563	5,683	-	193
1930	4,847	510	5,357	-	160
1931	-	-	4470	1	210
1932	3324	413	3737	6	147
1933	3438	383	3821	6	116
1934	5776	461	6237	6	118
1935	4,380	632	5,012	6	130
1936	4,937	632	5,569	6	151
1937	5,672	762	6,434	6	195
1938	6,092	575	6667	6	155
1939	-	-	6,079	7	-
1940	-	-	6,292	-	-
1941	-	-	6,545	-	-
1942	-	-	7,766	-	-
1943	-	-	9,057	-	-
1944	-	-	11,075	-	-
1945	-	-	11,968	-	-

Sources : Compiled by author from annual reports

Economic improvement by 1934 led many people to return to school and enrolment started rising in Mission schools. From four primary schools in 1934, the Mission had seven others by 1937 and by 1939 they had 15. When World War II ended in 1945, the colonial administration recognised 68 of the Basel Mission primary schools. The demand for schools had become so high that at least one primary school was opened each year. Many traditional rulers requested for the Mission to open schools in their villages. Some were created before the buildings were even constructed. Meanwhile, some shared the same building with the church, although most villages generally built their schools and asked the Mission for teachers.

The Mission also developed an attitude of self-help in the local congregations. The people of each locality contributed to the construction of the school in their area either through financing or by supplying materials. For example, in 1935, the Victoria congregation contributed £263 for a school building. Similarly, the Bafut parish helped to finance the building of their school. Then Government started giving grants for school buildings. In 1938, out of £1,315 subvention, £415 (approximately 32% of total Government grants) was allocated for school construction.

The high demand for schooling brought a greater burden on the Mission and from 1937 three types of schools emerged. These included the Village Schools, then the Parish Schools (which depended on the Mission and the local communities), and the Assisted Schools that received Government assistance. Whereas this last category of schools was inspected and supervised by the Education Department and the Mission Education Board, the second one depended on the Home Board for directives, while the first depended on the parish community. This diversity of school systems rendered the achievement of a coherent Mission educational policy unattainable.

It is for this reason that in 1937, the Field Missionaries proposed that the finances be centralized so that government grants, school fees, revenues from work rendered by pupils, money and donations from the Home Board and other sources might all be placed and managed from a central treasury. This proposal was approved in 1938 by the Home Board. As regards leadership, it was considered that educational responsibilities had become too heavy and important to be merged with evangelical work in one person. Hence there was a separation of responsibilities. Fritz Raaflaub who was then serving his second tour in Cameroon was made the first Inspector of Basel Mission Education.

FIGURE 5.2. Fritz Raaflaub, veteran inter-war-years educator

Raaflaub was enthusiastic and determined to improve upon Basel Mission education. His first ambition was to eliminate competition between the different parishes and improve the building structures of the schools. He also wanted to institute equality among all Parish Schools. He paid initial attention to schools regularly visited by government administrators. Then he decided on a uniform curriculum for all schools in addition to recommended standard textbooks for all schools.

Finally, he embarked on the training and retraining of Basel Mission teachers so as to improve on their qualities. These reforms gave a clearer perspective to Basel Mission education and established hope for a better future.

This upward and better trend of Raflaud's reforms was halted by the outbreak of the Second World War in 1939. German nationals had resumed activities in their plantations at the Coast in 1925 because the new British colonizers failed to find British business people to buy the plantations. Harry Rudin argues that at the outbreak of the Second World War, there were more Germans in British Southern Cameroons than the English population in the territory.

German nationals in the territory were expelled at the onset of World War II. By 1940 the Basel Mission was left with only six (Swiss nationals) of the seventy Missionaries in the pre-war years. Raflaub was given additional responsibility by being ordained a pastor to fill the gap created by departing German pastors. He had to handle both educational and evangelical responsibilities. However, unlike what had happened during the previous war, the Government showed more concern for Mission education. Government promise of allocating money from the Colonial Welfare and Development Fund (CWDF) for school grants gave hope to Mission education. By 1942 the new procedure for offering Government grants eliminated the earlier distinction between assisted and non-assisted schools. These grants improved the finances of the Missions and became invariably an important source of their revenue.

Teachers were motivated through a salary increase to serve the Mission. Increased support from the Native Authority and local communities further helped in the building of classrooms and even in the payment of teachers. This way, the mandate period ended with a structured school system and encouraging enrolments as indicated in table 5.1 above.

Trusteeship to Postcolonial Period

The post-war educational objective in Cameroon aimed at mass education at the primary level and the development of post primary education. The Basel Mission did not hesitate to take advantage of government disposition in school provisions to pursue evangelical and educational objectives. At the same time, the Field Missionaries increasingly gained more autonomy from the Home Board and were confident of exploiting the situation to expand their education. And these Field Missionaries became conscious of the need to adequately prepare the indigenes for eventual independence.

They improved the provision of primary education and embarked on the development of teacher training, as well as secondary and vocational education in order to have an educated Christian population on whom the church could be built. Events relating to the Mission during the Second World War reminded them of their earlier expulsion and delayed return after the First World War and the impact on their work. These reminiscences impacted on them to prepare competent indigenous Cameroonians to eventually replace the Missionaries, in case of a recurrence of a disintegrating situation.

As earlier indicated, the demand for more schools in all villages where the Mission extended its evangelical campaign remained high. The Mission had emerged from the war with a total of 68 primary schools, an enrolment of 5,155 pupils and a total of 200 teachers. With the exception of the girls' school in Victoria, all the schools had African headmasters by 1940. For evangelical reasons, primary education remained the targeted sector.

The demand for primary schools as against Vernacular Schools was increasing since most people looked forward to fitting themselves in the modern economy and vernacular education did not adequately prepare its graduates for this attractive sector. The government subsequently took measures to stop vernacular education, not so much because of the nature of education, but rather because of local prejudices associated with ethnic groups whose languages were used in these schools; many people of non-Douala and Bali origins were becoming more and more unwilling to study in Douala and Mungaka. However, the Basel Mission continued to offer vernacular education until the achievement of independence as indicated in the table (4) below.

Table 5.2. Decline of Vernacular Schools Enrolments during the Postwar Era

Year	Vernacular	Primary Schools	Total enrolment
1940	5,030	1,262	6,292
1945	6,813	5,155	11,968
1947	4,522	5,841	10,363
1951	1,169	8,223	9,392
1954	652	10,426	11,078
1956	568	14,032	14,600
1959	191	19,880	20,071

Source: Annual Reports and Reports to the United Nations Trusteeship Council

The post-war government education policies had effects on Basel Mission education, accounting for the pattern of its development. In 1949, the first post-war education policy was promulgated. Government grants to primary schools depended on the qualifications of teachers. Since most of the Basel Mission schools were poorly staffed, the policy disfavoured them. This restriction added to the exclusion of German Missionaries during the post-war period to pose problems of staffing. This led to a steady dwindling of enrolment from 1949 to 1954, as indicated on table 5 below.

These problems became more noticeable because the Mission focused greater attention on the development of post-primary education from 1947. However, from 1954, when political and socio-economic situations improved, primary school enrolment regained momentum, as indicated in Table 5.3 below.

Table 5.3. BM Schools Enrolment in the Decolonization Period (1945-1966

Year	Enrolment	Year	Enrolment
1945	11.968	1956	14.600
1946	11.291	1957	15.978
1947	10.563	1958	17.163
1948	9.705	1959	20.071
1949	10.400	1960	25.042
1950	9.694	1961	-
1951	9.592	1962	30.870
1952	8.920	1963	34.641
1953	9.736	1964	-
1954	11.331	1965	40.845
1955	12.785	1966	49.392

Sources: Annual reports and statistics of education in West Cameroon

Teacher Training

The development of primary education depended upon the improvement of teachers' qualifications. Sir Sydney Philipson's Report of 1948 on education in Nigeria recommended the criteria for administering grants to be based on teachers' qualifications. This influenced the Missions to develop their own teacher training institutions. The idea of training teachers at Nyasoso to teach and catechize, as practiced under German rule, was not welcomed by most Cameroonians. Hence in 1944, a one-year Preliminary Teacher Training Centre (PTTC) was started in Nyasoso.

In 1947, the institution was converted into a two-year Elementary Teachers Training Centre (ETTC) and transferred to Bali, leaving the Nyasoso Centre for the exclusive training of catechists. In 1949, the college was transferred to Batibo to give room for the establishment of a secondary school in Bali.

FIGURE 5.3. Basel Mission Teachers Training College Batibo

FIGURE 5.4. Basel Mission Teachers Training College Nyasoso (founded in 1963)

The Teacher Training Centre was started by Rev. J. Grest and on the staff was Solomon Tandeng Muna who later became an eminent political figure in Cameroon.

FIGURE 5.5. Hon Solomon Tandeng Muna

The Batibo Teacher Training College was a great achievement of the post-war period. It rapidly supplied the Mission with the required trained teachers whose presence attracted government recognition and financial grants. By 1952 the Mission could already boast of 194 certificated teachers whose salaries were paid by the government. Since the policy also stipulated that experienced non-certificated teachers could be partly paid by the state, the Mission had in all 229 teachers receiving government financial assistance by 1952. By 1959 the college had one preliminary teacher's class and two classes of the elementary section. Since local languages were not taught in the regular schools, there was emphasis on good English during the training. In 1960, oral English became part of the curriculum and was examined at the end of the course. While the Mission received appreciable support from the Government to train their teachers, a significant problem was still pending in the training of female teachers.

Female Education

The Basel Mission, like all other missionary societies and providers of education in Cameroon before the Second World War, had paid little attention to female education. Girls' education was first raised as an important problem in 1929. Missionary ladies were posted to open girls' schools in Victoria, Buea and Bali. But these ladies taught the girls only domestic science and religious instruction. Only Victoria had a school building for girls by 1931.

Until 1951 the Victoria school served both as a boarding and day school while still emphasizing domestic science education. From that year it became a full day school. Meanwhile, from 1941 it had been reorganised to function as a full primary school with English as the language of instruction. The headmistress was always a European until 1951 when Catherine Lyonga took over. The first African male staff was Abraham Ngole who eventually became the first Basel Mission Cameroonian church leader, the Moderator of the Church. An attempt to start a girls' school in Mbengwi by 1934 failed and was transferred to Bafut in 1937, and then converted into a boarding school. The events of the Second World War caused its closure, as the Missionary ladies were expelled from Cameroon.

Government and Mission concern for girls' education after the war resulted in the re-opening of the Bafut girls' school in 1947 by Lina Weber who became popularly known and has remained fondly remembered as "Na Weber".

She eventually became the architect of girls' education for the Basel Mission. Na Weber was initially assisted in the school by Mfobe Fusi. Together with him, they developed the school into a full primary school by 1949, attracting Basel Mission school girls from many parts of the country.

In addition to these two schools in Victoria and Bafut, many girls registered in the co-educational schools of the Basel Mission all over the country. The increasing number of primary school girls created the problem of supplying female teachers. The Mission trained their girls in Nigeria but most parents were reluctant to release their daughters to go that far. When the Roman Catholic Mission opened the first Girls' Teacher Training College in Kumba (Saint Francis Teachers' Training College) in 1951, it started absorbing some of the Basel Mission girls. From 1954 when Southern Cameroons revolted against Nigerian political control and gained quasi autonomy, Southern Cameroons students became hesitant to attend Nigerian schools. Thus, the only training centre available to Basel Mission school girls was the Catholic institution in Kumba. Inter-denominational rivalry motivated the Basel Mission moves to establish a training college. There was fear of conversion of the Basel Mission girls into Catholicism, besides the growing demand for many more female teachers eligible for grants from the Government.

FIGURE 5.6. (Lina Weber) Na Weber, driving force of B.M. female education Mission

The Basel Mission could have established a Female Teachers' Training College by 1956, if they were not expecting Government's promise to support them start one, together with a girls' secondary school in collaboration with the Baptist Mission. Instead, Government support was given to the Catholic Mill Hill Mission to open the first girls' secondary school (Queen of the Holy Rosary Secondary School, Okoyong – Mamfe) in 1956.

Structural changes were also introduced. In November 1957, the Basel Mission granted independence to the indigenous Church, which became known as the Presbyterian Church in Southern Cameroons – now the Presbyterian Church in Cameroon, abbreviated as PCC. But the Basel Mission continued to assist the new Church, managing schools and Medical services for it until 1968 when the Mission withdrew.

The Basel Mission and the new Church were enthused by the need for female education, especially at the threshold of independence from colonial administration. In 1960 the Mission appealed to government for authorization to establish a female teacher training college and were given a grant for an Elementary Teachers' Training College. That is how a teacher training college came about in Mankon-Bamenda, known as Women's Teacher Training College (WTTC). This school first started in January 1961 at a temporary site in the Girls' School at Bafut under Na Weber as its pioneer principal. The school helped in supplying the trained female teachers that the Mission and the Church needed at independence.

Teacher training by the Mission was limited to the training of teachers of elementary classes while Higher Elementary Teachers' Training was offered by the government at the GTTC, in Kumba. Owing to the large number of applications from all Missions into the Government College, it became necessary for Government to authorise and support the establishment of Mission teachers' training colleges to train higher elementary teachers. This grade of teachers was the highest for primary schools. They taught the final-year classes of the primary school and junior classes of secondary schools. Secondary school leavers were also admitted at this level of training to develop careers in teaching.

The Basel Mission started offering Teachers' Grade Two courses in January 1962 and in 1963 they graduated the first batch of 30 students. Financial constraints led to the beginning of co-educational training at the Higher Elementary College in Batibo. The Grade Three graduates of WTTC Mankon continued their training for Grade Two in Batibo. Thus, at the close of Basel Mission educational activities in 1966, they had set up a well-structured training scheme for teachers to cope with the increasing demand for primary school teachers.

Secondary Education

The establishment of many primary schools suggested the need for post primary education. Both the Government and the Mission were pressured by the population for the establishment of a secondary school. In 1940 the Basel Mission Inspector proposed to convert the Middle School in Nyasoso into a Junior Secondary School or a "Full Middle School" so as to avoid the idea of letting primary school graduates from Basel Mission schools to enrol in the Roman Catholic Secondary School opened at Sasse in 1939. Between 1938 and 1940, the Missionaries urged Basel Mission children to register in Nyasoso but the children and their parents were in search of regular secondary education which was only available in Sasse.

Fear of losing their adherents forced the Basel Mission to take the expensive alternative measure of enrolling their pupils in Hope Wadel secondary school, Calabar, Nigeria. This measure proved financially too expensive for the Mission. After several exchanges of letters between the Missionaries in Cameroon and the Home Board at Basel, an agreement on the establishment of a Basel Mission Secondary School was reached in Basel in 1947. Further discussions followed and a common entrance examination was conducted in Cameroon in 1948. Fifty-three candidates were selected and school started officially in February 1949 at Bali, with D.H. O'Neil as the first principal, assisted by

J.P. Schneider and J.A. Ozimba, the first African staff member.

FIGURE 5.7. D. H. O'Neil, Pioneer Principal BM College

FIGURE 5.8. J.A. Ozimba, pioneer Senior African Tutor, Basel Mission College, Bali (1949-1957)

FIGURE 5.9. Current main block of CPC Bali

FIGURE 5.10. Image Dr. & Mrs Peter Rudin-Principal, (extreme left and right) with Mr & Mrs Donald Whitt – Vice Principal (middle)

The school curriculum comprised Cambridge overseas schools examination subjects. In 1952, the Principal realized from the political developments in the country that French was eventually going to be a necessity to the boys because he foresaw a reunification of the British and French Cameroons in the near future. He therefore dropped Latin from the curriculum and replaced it with French. The foresightedness of the college authorities to introduce French this early prepared the students for privileged national positions when the French and the British sectors re-united in 1961.

General science was also started in Form One. In 1957, the new principal, Dr. Peter Rudin, revised the curriculum. He replaced General science with Chemistry and Biology and later added Physics. The curriculum therefore included: English Language, English Literature, French, Mathematics, Additional Mathematics, Geography, History, Biology, Chemistry, Physics and Religious Knowledge. In the lower classes Art and Music were also taught.

Extracurricular activities included games, athletics, swimming and gardening. Club activities included scouting, boxing, debate, British constitution, current events, nature study, etiquette, drama, photography, and stamp collection. The first batch graduated in December 1953. On 13 March 1954, the first Cambridge schools certificate examination result was released and 19 out of 20 candidates passed, an excellence maintained in subsequent years. From 1955 the Government requested the Basel Mission to jointly run a double stream in the school with the Cameroon Baptist Convention. By June 1956 both Missions agreed on the joint sponsorship of the college and it changed its name from Basel Mission College to Cameroon's Union College. It was in June 1957 that the first two Baptist staff members joined the college. In October, final arrangements changed the name to Cameroon Protestant College Bali (CPC) and the double stream started in January 1958. The college enrolment increased again and by 1960 there were 233 students. That year, only 64 candidates were selected out of 800 applicants. Further pressure on

Basel Mission for more Secondary Schools led to the opening of one in Kumba (1962) and another in Besongabang (1964), both co-educational.

CPC served as the training ground for administrators of the newly opened secondary schools. Cable Walters, a British volunteer who served for many years as a Chemistry teacher in CPC, was sent to open the Secondary school (Basel Mission College) in Kumba. Norman Haupt, an American Baptist Missionary then serving as Vice Principal in CPC was sent to open the Baptist Secondary school (Joseph Merrick College) in Ndu. Later, he became principal of Saker Baptist College in Victoria. Miss Schultz, an American Missionary who was teaching in CPC, also proceeded to Saker Baptist College as principal. Donald Witt, who was also Vice Principal in CPC, later became principal of Saker Baptist College in Victoria. Samuel Mbong Eseh, one of the pioneer students of the school who subsequently served as History and sports teacher in CPC, also moved to the Secondary School (Basel Mission College) in Besongabang as principal. Subsequently, ATM Mofor who served in CPC as a Geography teacher also moved to Besongabang as principal. Records on these school administrators of the new secondary schools demonstrate that they had gained from their experiences in CPC and that they established some of the ethical values of CPC in the new schools.

Vocational/Technical Education

Apart from general education, the Basel Mission offered other forms of education. Vocational education was given to both boys and girls, but apparent lack of interest towards it characterized both parents and students. The government too demonstrated lack of motivation, which discouraged the Mission from expanding the scale of provision. The tanning of hides and skins scheme begun in Nyasoso in the 1930s, for example, failed to receive assistance from government.

The Mission also established Youth Centres in the main towns that offered opportunities to school drop-outs to continue their education through evening classes and distance learning courses. These centres also provided facilities for the development of talents in drama, music and sports. Handicraft training centres aimed at developing local crafts from wood, fibre and metal were established at Bafut and Bali. In addition, the Mission opened Rural Training Centres (RTC) in Kumba and Fonta for training in carpentry, bricklaying, plumbing, farming and animal husbandry.

Meanwhile, the Mission's bookshop and printing press in Victoria provided invaluable support to education in terms of supplying learning and teaching materials. The bookshop was originally only in Victoria during the German colonial rule. After the war, the Mission revived the printing press and bookshop in 1929. In 1950 a bookshop was opened in Kumba, then another one was established in Bamenda in 1952, and yet another in Tiko in 1954. The one in Mamfe was opened in 1957. Throughout the colonial period, the Basel Mission was the main supplier of all reading and writing materials in the country because of the printing press and the bookshop.

The Handing-Over

Having in the above main ways contributed to the Cameroon educational development, the Basel Mission in 1968 handed over 260 primary schools with an enrolment of 49,392 pupils, assessed as 32.9 per cent of primary school enrolment in West Cameroon. In these schools were 1,414 primary school teachers. They also handed over three secondary schools which by 1965 had a total enrolment of 601 students and a staff of 30, besides three teacher training institutions with 469 students taught by 27 teachers by 1965.

The Mission handed over to the PCC a well-structured school administration system. The entire educational system was headed by the Education Secretary who was assisted by two Supervisors of schools covering the Forest and the Grassland zones respectively. There were also 14 managers of schools, each school having a headteacher. At the helm of this administrative structure were the Education Committee and its Standing Committee which met regularly to ensure the proper management of the schools.

The Mission had developed a careful Africanisation policy after the Second World War that prepared Cameroonians to handle these responsibilities. The financial assistance of the Government and private enterprises, such as the Cameroon Development Corporation, helped the Mission to train Cameroonians who eventually took over responsibilities from the Basel Mission. The evangelical activities were handed over in 1957 to an indigenous Presbyterian Church in Cameroon led by Rev. Ngole as the first Moderator. By 1968, when the schools were being handed over, most of the managerial posts were already filled by Cameroonians. Thus, the Basel Mission left a clear structure that enabled the new church, Presbyterian Church in Cameroon, to continue contributing to Cameroon education. But whether the pattern of education accounts for postcolonial education problems is a matter for debate.

Basel Mission education operated under different regimes and circumstances, and, despite its distinct educational system, it was constrained by Government subventions to conform to the policies of the ruling governments. Government funds, especially during the post-war period, sponsored Mission education. The grants paid for the construction of Mission school buildings, salaries of teachers, purchase of some school equipment, and scholarships to students and workers of the Mission were paid by the government. Such assistance deserved collaboration from the Mission in return.

Nationalism during the post-war period and African aspiration for development on the Western model also contributed enormously to determine the pattern of education. The school curricula were British and the few books written on Cameroon and Africa were published by non-Africans. When Vernacular Schools were stopped, the teaching of Cameroon culture through the application of local languages stopped as well. Swiss Missionaries involved with education took British examinations to qualify to teach in Southern Cameroons. All post-primary school teachers and school administrators received training in Britain or in other British colonies such as Nigeria or the Gold Coast. Thus, British culture dominated.

The Basel Mission Home Board reduced its involvement in educational policies, especially from 1957, and sought rather to offer support to the new church. The Missionaries made all efforts to understand the British educational system. Thus the British education pattern prevailed and imbued those who went through it with British culture, which remains their model.

The Basel Mission's relations with other Christian Missions might also account for some of the postcolonial education problems. There were only three Christian Missions (Catholic Mission, Baptist Mission and Basel Mission). The accelerated rate of school expansion in the post-war and post-independence periods inevitably placed these Missions into competition. Each Missionary society had the primary objective of gaining more Cameroonian adherents through education. They ultimately had to compete through the creation of schools for adherents. They fought also to obtain Government grants in order to extend into new areas and to sustain what they had achieved. These rivalries had an impact on education. Villages and districts were associated with specific Missions or denominations. As such, seeds of disagreement were planted.

Perhaps more disturbing was the impact of these differences on political inclinations. It was, and still is, the belief that the presence of an influential political figure belonging to a particular denomination invariably favours members of that denomination. For instance, the Education Secretary for the Basel Mission was disillusioned by the failure of Honourable S.T. Muna and Honourable Ndamukong to influence the government to assist the Mission in the opening of a Secondary School in Mbengwi in 1964.

It was also thought that the opening of the Catholic Secondary Schools in Mankon, Njinikom and Banso in that same year (1964) resulted from the influence of political figures like

J.N. Foncha, the then Vice President of the Federal Republic of Cameroon and Prime Minister of West Cameroon, A.N. Jua, and Honourable Lafon, who were formerly teachers with the Catholic Mission. Politicians also found that their constituencies and the Christians within these constituencies could support them if they influenced the establishment of schools. This practice had significant implications on the development of education.

It is clear that German and British colonial education in Cameroon was predominantly provided and supervised by Missionary societies. Meanwhile, the French colonial education was largely controlled by the government. The differences between these two colonial legacies considerably account for the difficulties involved in harmonising both systems. More importantly, the differences in French and British colonial education policies towards private education have had an appreciable impact on postcolonial educational developments.

The Basel Mission's sustained feeling was that the British colonial government did not treat them as fairly as other Missionary Societies. They felt that the Catholic Mill Hill Mission was more favoured because of their British connection, and the Baptists because of their Anglo-American background. Thus, their German connection affected their relations with the British colonial government. This attitude was inherited by the new Cameroonian church leaders. For example, they questioned why the Basel Mission with 30,870 pupils in primary schools by 1962 could not be permitted to have more than one secondary school while sharing another one with the Baptists. This argument was raised because the Catholic Mission enrolled 38,443 pupils and was allowed to run three secondary schools while the Baptists enrolled 12,111 pupils and were permitted to have the same number of secondary schools as the Basel Mission.

However, a more plausible explanation for government's attitude might be discerned from the Basel Mission education policy. Whereas the other Missions established and maintained fewer and better organised schools, all the time adhering strictly to the government regulations that determined the award of grants, the Basel Mission was divided between the policy of pleasing their village communities (by keeping less organised Vernacular Schools with unqualified staff) and failing to satisfy government regulations. Well-organised schools did not only attract government support, they also attracted more pupils. This partially explains why the Basel Mission lost the leading position in enrolments, which they had held under the Germans.

The assumption that the Basel Mission education could have prospered more under the Germans but for their defeat at the war remains arguable too. The increasing German nationalism and overbearing desire for world conquest at the eve of the First World War, which contradicted the principles for which the Basel Mission stood, were already having profound effects on the Mission's relations with the regime by 1911. Thus the situation of the Basel Mission under a victorious German colonial rule might not have been any different.

CHAPTER SIX

CAMEROONIAN REACTIONS TO BASEL MISSION EDUCATION DURING THE BRITISH REGIMES

Cameroonian reasons for attending schools, whether Missionary or non-Missionary varied, but most were related to well-defined political, social, or economic goals. Really, few Cameroonians attended Mission schools for the sake of their eschatological message because their spiritual needs were well-provided for in their traditional belief systems. As such, like elsewhere, African interests in education occasionally conflicted with those of the Missionary societies.

The Missionaries placed religion at the forefront of the school curriculum because, to them, education detached from its religious moorings was valueless. Meanwhile, Cameroonians asked for more utilitarian subjects on the curricula to enable them to have access to the European economy. The different perceptions of the role of school by both the Missionaries, on the one hand, and their Cameroonian clientele, on the other, underpin the reactions of Cameroonians during the colonial era. The tension resulting from the conflicting opinions of education must have influenced African attitudes towards education in general and to Missionary education in particular. All considered, the assumption that Africans resisted the introduction of education and were non-contributory to educational development is debatable. The inter-relationships and interactions that developed from the Mission education invariably influenced the formation of attitudes to education and consequently are implicit in the post-colonial educational development.

With the exception of the later part of the French colonial rule when state control became more significant, Cameroon education, as earlier stated, was dominated by Missionary societies. These societies brought with them not only religious values but their cultures, which were transmitted implicitly through education. Both aspects were important in determining the pattern of Missionary education. The pseudo-scientific "facts" placing Africans at the backward stage of human development, which generated debate on the educability of the African in the nineteenth and early twentieth centuries, also influenced colonial and Missionary perceptions of the Africans, determining the type of education considered appropriate for Africans. Inevitably, colonial officials and Missionaries disagreed at times on matters of African political and educational policies but, more frequently, Missionaries actively encouraged the extension of imperial control which unavoidably provoked African reactions.

The establishment and expansion of Basel Mission education during the colonial period and in the postcolonial period (more especially the latter) could not have been accomplished without the contributions of some Cameroonians and their active participation. Missionary education may therefore be considered a joint effort of Europeans and Cameroonians. The notion of Cameroonian reactions might trigger a debate on the representativeness, i.e., the proportion of the population or the group involved. True, the proportion of Cameroonians involved in education until independence remained small, but the number of people involved in reactions against European institutions outnumbered this group, enhanced by the pattern of social organization being centralized or acephalous, and on leadership skills. Underpinning all reactions were the interests of the leaders in particular and the society in general.

Although this study refers to "Cameroonian reactions", not all Cameroonians reacted in the same way at the same time. Some welcomed Western education; others rejected it; and still others (it must be remarked here) were no doubt undecided or indifferent, particularly if they were far removed from the centres of educational and evangelical action. Their differentiated reactions depended on the utility or the importance of education and their exposure to it. To the common man, education was inseparable from all other European institutions.

Under the British rule during the League of Nations Mandate and the United Nations Trusteeship, Cameroonians kept demanding for more access to education. Their enthusiasm for schooling was demonstrated in their willingness to participate in the development and support of Mission schools. While the joint administration of British Cameroons with Nigeria might have delayed the development of education, it stimulated the development of nationalism, which. significantly affected education. The inception of British rule had raised great expectations due to the Cameroonian foreknowledge of British culture (as experienced in the pre-colonial era from the London Baptist Missionary education) and the English cultural impact (derived from British trading firms in Cameroon coastal towns). But this nostalgia for English culture met with a nonchalant British response in the post-war period, particularly as regards education. This nonchalance is obvious when it is considered that apart from some unapproved Mission Vernacular schools operated by some Cameroonians, access to education was limited to only six Government schools until 1922 when 12 Native Administration Infant Schools were created. Yet, Cameroonians who had schooled under the Germans, and were interested in continuing or enrolling their children, demanded for more schooling opportunities.

The Cameroonian-sponsored schools provoked sociopolitical problems that caused wide resentment, particularly amongst traditional leaders. The administration reported in 1924 that servants in royal palaces reacted against the rulers following the notion of freedom imbibed from Western education. For this reason, some of the traditional rulers rose against the existence of the schools. The limited access to education was further stifled by the introduction of school fees. Discontentment was demonstrated from 1922 to 1924 against the exaction of school fees, as well as the building and maintenance of school structures. Rutherford, who was the administrative officer for Mamfe, attributed the declining enrolment in schools to "a genuine reaction against the neglect of the people".

In spite of these reactions, Cameroonian desire for Western education remained high. Captain Denton, the administrative officer for Victoria observed: "...the thirst for knowledge is increasing not for the sake of knowledge so much as for the pecuniary benefits and social prestige which it is hoped will accrue there from."[22]

Thus, the reaction was not against education, but rather for better conditions and greater access to schooling. Apparently, Nigerian anti-colonial protests influenced Cameroonians and led them to organise themselves and present their grievances to the government. From the early 1930s, the ideas of Herbert Macauley of the Nigerian National Democratic Party (NNDP) influenced Cameroonians to form the Cameroon Welfare Union (CWU), which aimed at educating all other Cameroonians about the problems of development and to pressurize the Government for reforms. In 1937, a delegation of CWU met with the Director of Education and presented their complaints about education in the territory. They asked for more primary schools and more training facilities for teachers as well as the establishment of a Government secondary school. That contact influenced the establishment of a secondary school in Sasse near Buea in 1939.

Events during the Second World War further strengthened the Cameroonian case against the British regime. For Cameroonian soldiers during the war had corresponded with the Resident, specifically on the issue of development, influenced by the level of advancement they observed while fighting abroad. From their earnings at the war front, these soldiers made pledges and even sent home contributions in cash towards development projects. They insisted on the importance of improving the quality and quantity of education. Since education during the British rule

22 1924 Annual Report.

was indirectly provided by the Missionary societies, it became incumbent on the Basel Mission to rethink their strategies in the provision of schools.

Cameroonians from the French zone also significantly impacted on the people's attitude towards British policy. Although Cameroon evolved *under* two colonial regimes, unofficial contacts between the two territories were regular. During periods of oppression in the French zone, for example there was a massive exodus of French speaking Cameroonians into the British territory. Particularly, during the period of railway extension and road construction, when forced and unpaid labour was imposed in the French territory, many migrated to the British sector where they settled permanently. Some found paid employment in the German plantations within the British zone. It is reported that of the 12,128 labourers in the plantations within the British Cameroons by 1926, there were 6,330 people from the French zone, constituting over 52% of the working population. It is from this working class that the highest demand for education came. The number of French Cameroonians remained significant throughout the colonial period and in 1960, repressive measures against terrorism led to over 5,000 more fleeing into British Southern Cameroons.

Among these people were some who had special desire for British culture and education such as R.J.K. Dibonge. They were interested in the development of education for their children. They became the driving force in the quest for British education. Despite the influence of the French Cameroonians, however, the British Cameroonian demands and protests never at any moment attained the explosive dimension noticed under the French administration. This might be attributed to the administrative system which avoided repression and the educational system given by the missionaries who insisted on religious virtues.

Yet, similarities in the formation of protest groups can be identified. Several trade unions and development associations formed on the basis of common ethnic or village backgrounds led by graduates of Mission schools were established immediately after the world war in the British zone. Some of the prominent associations included: the Bakweri Development Union, the Bamenda Improvement Association and the Mamfe Improvement Association. The transformation of all the German plantations into a single company, known as the Cameroon Development Corporation, led to the establishment of a large trade union, Cameroon Development Corporation Workers' Union (CDCWU). The returning soldiers from the war front also established the Kamerun Ex-servicemen National Union (KENU).

All these associations had nationalist tendencies masterminded by graduates of Mission schools, with the demand for education being topmost in their programmes. During the visit of Elliot's Commission on higher education in the colonies in 1943, those that were already in existence combined forces to produce a memorandum on education in British Cameroons. The memorandum referred to the promise made by the Director of Education in 1937 and reminded the government that

> ...at present any Cameroonian wishing to obtain education higher than standard six, because of lack of room in the Roman Catholic Mission College at Sasse, must go to Nigeria, a procedure which because of insufficient means, the majority are loath to adopt and, as a result, the local educational standard is low and most of the higher government posts are therefore held by Nigerians.[23]

The memorandum was signed by representatives of all the associations, including; J.M. Williams, member of the Legislative Council of Nigeria representing Cameroon, S.M. Ngoo, president of the Cameroon Welfare Union and E.M.L. Endeley, Chairman of the Cameroon Youth League. Once more, their central thrust was education, particularly post primary education.

---

23 NAE. Ab/a 1932/7 Cameroon Memorandum of Evidence before the Eliot Commission, 1943.

They indicated that

> ...out of the large number of children leaving school in this period only about two percent had advantage of any secondary education of any sort; and out of this frightfully small number, only about 0.8% proceeds beyond form IV (the limit of Sasse College) by entering secondary schools in Nigeria.[24]

Their emphasis was on the development of secondary education so as to raise people who could be trained to fill higher government posts. They blamed the predominance of Nigerians in the civil service appointments within the territory as indicated in table 6.1 to low access to education in Cameroon. Only 80 Cameroonians out of an estimated population of 500,000 people could have places in the civil service. Recruitment into this grade, like all other grades of the civil service, depended entirely on educational qualifications. Thus the inadequate provision of education was evidently the obstacle to Cameroonian aspirations to participate in the development of their own country. From the data in the table below, Missions provided more but government had better quality education.

Based on this evidence, which showed Government schools as being much better than the other schools and assuming that the quality of the teachers contributed to the results, the elite requested for more teacher training schools and the upgrading of the existing one into a full Higher Elementary Teachers' Training College. The result was the establishment of two Mission Teachers' Training Colleges and the upgrading of the Government College at Kumba into a full higher elementary teacher training centre.

Ultimately, Government sponsorship of the Missions to open training centres was influenced by the elites. But the persistent problem that the Missions were facing with teachers trained in

---

24 ibid.

the government training centre had its role. The tendency for such teachers (trained in the government training centres) was to abandon the Mission schools after training, in search for better paid jobs with the Government or elsewhere. Therefore, the opening of Mission Teacher Training Centres gave the Missions the opportunity to train their own teachers thereby guaranteeing greater commitment from the trained teachers.

Table 6.1. 1943 Elementary Schools Results per Agency

Agency	No of Schools	Entrants	Full Passes	Trial Passes	% Passes
Government	5	122	52	19	58.19
Native Authority	15	218	47	44	41.74
Missions	36	768	235	106	44.40
Total	59	1.048	334	169	47.99

Source: NAE Sb/a 1932/7, Cameroon Memorandum of Evidence before the Elliot Commission, 1943

The elite, blaming the backwardness of the territory on the slow and inadequate provision of education, asked for two secondary schools for boys to be located in the two distinct geographical regions of the grassland and forest regions. They also asked for a secondary school for girls to be built mid-way between the two regions. In the fourth place, they requested for more teacher training colleges and the upgrading of existing ones to train teachers for all the levels of the primary school. Their requests demonstrated a strong acceptance of education and a highly motivated desire for elitist education because the issue of technical and professional education was not addressed.

As already mentioned, Government response to the memorandum and subsequent pressures was the creation of the Basel Mission Teacher Training College at Nyassoso and the establishment of the Basel Mission secondary school in Bali. Although these institutions belonged to the Mission, the Government contributed substantially in financing them. The maintenance and payment of Mission teachers during the post-war period was also largely done by the Government.

CHAPTER SEVEN

BASEL MISSION EDUCATION TO PCC

Right from the beginning of the activities of the Basel Mission in Cameroon there were plans to eventually hand over missionary work to a local church in Cameroon. That is why it aimed at producing "educated African assistants", *Gehilfen*, who would eventually become Christian leaders (catechists, pastors, teachers, clerks, artisans, and technicians) for both church and state. Thus at the dawn of decolonization following the end of the Second World War, the Basel Mission started the process of handing over their work to Cameroonians. A cursory review of the process of devolution from Basel Mission to the local Church indicates three main stages.

Stage One

The first stage stretched from the establishment of the Mission in 1886 and lasted till the decolonization era. During this period, the Mission took full responsibility for the entire operation of missionary activities. The Mission alone decided on what was to be done, how it had to be done, when and where new Mission stations had to be built, schools established and the financing of all projects. The Cameroonian workers barely assisted the Missionaries and were termed "helpers" (*Gehilfen*).

Stage Two

The second stage started after the Second World War, when the Church Synod and Synod Councils were established and responsibilities gradually devolved from Mission to Cameroonian Church officers. At first, it was more for Church or spiritual matters and later in the placement of management personnel. At that initial state, Mission and Church existed side by side as two separate entities but correlated and even intertwined in varying degrees, with the Mission assuming most of the responsibility over personnel and finance. During this period too, Mission was in charge of all institutions of education and medical services, and all technical training. As far as the Ministry was concerned, there were more readily available Cameroonian staff to replace Europeans, although in areas such as medical service, there were hardly any available qualified personnel.

Stage Three

This final stage marked the full autonomy of the local Church over all work that the Basel Mission had established since 1886. All expatriates that had to continue serving in Cameroon were placed at the disposal of the Church Boards. Henceforth the Church assumed full responsibility over everything that the Mission was leaving behind. At the same time, legal instruments were established transferring all Mission institutions, land and property to the Church.

But at this final stage it was not easy for the Church to have the qualified and experienced manpower to replace all the expatriates. For this reason, negotiations were made for the Church to identify areas needing expatriate Missionaries and inform the Home Board to do the selection of qualified candidates for recruitment. So the Home Board had to continue assisting the Presbyterian Church in Cameroon for quite a while. But how prepared was the Church to shoulder the responsibilities inherited from the Mission?

Preparation of Cameroonian Church Leaders

The preparation of Cameroonian church workers was taken seriously throughout the period of the Basel Mission in Cameroon. This was particularly spurred by the problems suffered by the Church during the non-missionary years (1916 to 1925) when the Missionaries were expelled from the country and there were no competent locals to unite and lead the Church. The Mission therefore embarked on preparing local Church leaders when it resumed operation in 1925 and from 1934, the Mission began gradually to hand over responsibilities to competent Cameroonians. By 1940, for example, all headmasters of schools were Cameroonians with the exception of the girl's school in Victoria.

Events arising from the Second World War further influenced the preparation of the indigenous staffs of the Basel Mission to take over from the expatriates. To start with, all Missionaries of German origin were repatriated from Cameroon during the war. Only the Swiss missionaries were left. And even these were leaving, as Werner Keller reports: two Swiss missionaries returned to Switzerland in 1941 and two others followed in 1943, all for health reasons (W. Keller, 1968:80). This seriously depleted the number of expatriate missionaries.

The Mission turned to the 10 ordained Cameroonian pastors. These are said to have worked with admirable courage and endurance with the few missionaries that were left to sustain Church work. Encouraged by the input of the Cameroonian pastors, the missionaries offered more responsibilities to Cameroonians. In 1946, in spite of the fact that more missionaries had come into Cameroon, the Rev. E. Peyer suggested the appointment of a chairman. Subsequently, Cameroonians took over the leadership. In 1950, therefore, the Rev. Peter Essoka Diso was appointed Chairman of the General Synod and the Rev. Jacob Shu was made the vice; District Synods, the Presbyteries and treasuries.

In 1949, Education Committees were established in each of the four divisions (Bamenda, Mamfe, Kumba, and Victoria) composed of Missionaries and Cameroonians. Then in 1955, a General Education Committee comprising members of both parties was established to take care of all educational matters.

FIGURE 7.1. The Rev. Peter Esoka, first Synod Chairman (Moderator)

Manager of schools. J. F. Mancho in 1960 was appointed to the same post. Meanwhile Eugene Ekiti was appointed Supervisor of schools for the Grassfields in 1959. Thus, before the declaration of independence in Southern Cameroons where the Mission was established, all the major posts in the Basel Mission education system were held by Church workers of Cameroon origin. However, although Basel Mission handed over all the evangelical activities to the Presbyterian Church in 1957, the educational and medical activities remained with the Basel Mission until 27th November 1968. For over a decade, there was preparation and training of Cameroonians for a progressive handover of the educational service of the Mission.

FIGURE 7.2. Jacob Shu, first Synod vice-chairman

FIGURE 7.3. Eugene Ekiti, pioneer Cameroonian Education Secretary

For a closer follow up of education, in 1954 J. T. Ebai and J. F. Mancho were appointed as Visiting Teachers for the Forest Region and the Grassfields Region respectively. Then in 1958, R. M. Ntoko, who was Visiting Teacher for Kumba, was appointed.

Handing-over of Schools

The Missionary Conference had made three requests starting from May 1961 to October 1963 for the transfer of schools to the Presbyterian Church. Twice the request was rejected outrightly by the Cameroonian members of the Committee. It was at the third submission in November 1963 that the General Synod Committee reluctantly accepted to study the proposal. According to a statement in a message to the Committee made by the Moderator of the Church, the Rt. Rev. A. Ngole, the Church was only going to accept the transfer because "they were convinced that God was calling the Church to take her share of responsibility in the Christian education of the future generations in Cameroon."

FIGURE 7.4. Rt. Rev. Abraham Ebong Ngole (1899-1980), First PCC Moderator

The Basel Mission had maintained the educational system for the Presbyterian Church since 1957 and had made significant changes. At the public handing over ceremony in the Buea stadium, witnessed by both civil and church dignitaries on 27th November 1968, the Field Secretary of the Basel Mission, Rev. Willy Bachman, handed the legal documents to Rev. Aaron Su, the Synod Clerk of the Presbyterian Church. Thereafter, the Presbyterian Church became the Proprietor of all the schools and institutions they had managed till then (see Table 7.1 below).

Table 7.1. BM Educational Establishments Handed Over to PCC

Type of Institution	1957
Primary schools	123
Primary school children	14,022
Secondary schools	1
Secondary school students	146
Teacher Training Colleges	1
Teachers in Training	52

Adopted from Werner Keller: The History of the Presbyterian Church, 1968 (p.120)

As the above table shows, there was a tremendous growth in education in the decade following the declaration of the autonomy of the Presbyterian Church in 1957. By 1967, the number of primary schools had more than doubled and the population of the school children more than tripled. There were three secondary schools as against just one in 1957 and the population of the students was about six times the number in 1957.

One of the major problems of schools in the pre-independence days had been the dearth of qualified teachers. The number of Teacher Training Colleges belonging to the Church rose from one with 52 student teachers in 1957 to 3 having 548 students in 1967. Thus the student teacher population was 10 times what was available in 1957. The creation of a female Teacher Training College in Mankon in 1961 and the functioning of a co-educational

Higher Elementary College in Batibo since 1964 were yet more laudable achievements during this transitional period. This enabled the Mission to have more female teachers. Another co-educational Teacher Training College was started in 1964 and in 1965, and it went operational in new buildings in Nyasoso. Mission had therefore made such tremendous strides that became a serious challenge to the Church. Will the Church be able to sustain the growth?

CONCLUSION

The place of Missionary education in the planting of Western education in Cameroon remains irrefutable. The difficulties that these Missionaries encountered in the attempt to open schools in difficult areas or in places that resisted European annexation can hardly be conjectured. It is therefore undeniably true, as upheld by H.W. Debrunner, that the educational foundation laid by Basel Mission was fundamentally important for the development of the country albeit there were many problems. For eighty-two years, this Missionary Society laboured hard to establish schools and other institutions in Cameroon under changing colonial regimes that sometimes were patronizing and at times antagonizing, and at other times simply indifferent to the Mission.

The Basel Mission left its indelible mark on the canvas of Cameroon's educational map. That mark should be the inspiration and guide to present-day education officials, both of the church and government. The errors should be shunned and the strong points honed to perfection. Native talent should be considered and local realities made the informing background of all syllabuses. And it may be that the Basel Mission past outlines the traps to avoid and the path to follow. Certain questions arise from its experience and worthy of evoking here for our edification and action:

The Basel mission in a foolhardy competition, opened up schools without the manpower or resources to run them, is it possible that missions, private non-denominational persons and even government have not learned from that error?

It put evangelization at the forefront of its educational programme and alienated those who valued their tradition and cultural practices; is it possible that some of our educational programmes are informed by less than objective knowledge?

The missionaries belittled the African and taught him to value European ways and less of African culture; how much is human dignity and freedom at the core of our educational programmes?

The Basel experience shows a lack of cooperation from the government in the propagation of technical schools; are there some practical skills and trades that would bloom if we took the time to consider, outline and engage as part of our educational programme?

The Basel Mission was surprised as it were by the ability of Africans to govern and run missionary institutions; for how long are we to undervalue the native talent of Cameroonians and help bring over Western and Eastern technologies or develop ours rather than forever being consumers of these technologies?

The embarrassments of the world wars took the missions off-guard; are our educational institutions made ready to quickly return to normal should there be similar disruptions?

The missions trained Cameroonians for administration and cared less about output in various fields, a phenomenon echoed in the attitude of laziness common among many of our countrymen; to what extent is our education certificate-oriented rather than production-bound?

These questions and more are pointers to the value of taking stock of the Basel Mission contribution to Cameroon's educational system, of making the best of it, not only by being informed on it, but also by engaging in righting its wrongs.

AFTERWORD

In the light of the many changes and challenges confronting Cameroon today, it is easy to forget or jumble up the past and focus on the present without a sense of direction. Where a thing begins, is often a pointer to where it is going and whether it will reach its destination. And so to make sense of the contemporary situation in Cameroon, it is its educational past that particularly merits meticulous documentation. And this merit is pitched on the value and status of education, for on education hangs all the accretions of modernity, development and even governance of Cameroon. This book vindicates most assertively Hans Kohn's view that historical research, like all scientific endeavour, carries its reward in the joy of discovering unknown facts, finding new interpretations and laying bare obscure relationships.

When it comes to that, the ponderous statement of fact is that the educational past of Cameroon hangs on the Basel Mission, which set itself on the foundations of the path-blazing British Baptists of 1844-1886. The Basel Mission set up thereafter as the mission that established, flourished, and even after changing its name, has become part of the very fabric of Cameroon's society. The Basel Mission educational system cannot therefore be overlooked, for it is the mirror of what the scratch-start and early basics looked like. It is the signpost of how developments have built on that beginning to shed educational, cultural and political life in Cameroon.

There is no denying that the British and American Baptists took their circumstantial parts in the evolution of the educational system of Cameroon; no denying that the Catholics played in time and availed themselves of advantages the Basel Mission hesitated to take or were denied; no denying that issues of rivalry forged unmanageable quandary of choices on the Basel Mission educational agenda; no denying that the various regimes (governments), from German to the French and English played their obstructing or supportive roles. These and more besides, it remains strongly verifiable that to the Basel Mission, more than any other, fell the onus of experimenting with educational policies, curriculum, teacher training models and educational programmes that had to include the core goal of evangelization while strategizing on having mission-trained hands in government positions.

In the attempt to face today's educational and other challenges it would be a disservice to the nation and Cameroon's educational system. From Basel Mission makeshift endeavours to cope with the challenges of the past, a lot of wisdom can be tapped with which to cater for the present stakes. And here in this volume Professor Mathew B. Gwanfogbe skillfully uncoils the processes that the mission followed, with punctual evidence of research, innovative interpretation, and keen analysis that betray an unwavering effort at exactitude. This painstaking endeavour is clinched by an insider's clarity on every point.

Subject matter, research method and analysis all considered, this work: *Basel Mission Education in Cameroon:1886-1968* — should be a desk copy manual for everyone, Cameroonian or freethinker the world over, interested in education, its history of growth and the challenges it raises even today.

N. Patrick Tata
Research and Editing Consultant

APPENDIX

Presbyterian Education Authority (PEA) Education Secretaries from 1968 to Date

SECRETARY	TERM OF OFFICE
Mr. Eugene A. Ekiti	1st September 1968 to 31st August 1986
Mr Abel N. Sumbele	1st September 1986 to 31st August 1994
Mr. Chrispus Tunyi	1st September 1994 to 4th December 1997
Mr. Baboni Joseph Che	1st January 1998 to 30th May 1998 acting
Mr. Baboni Joseph Che	1stJuly 1998 to 2nd July 2011
Mr. Njie Samuel Kale	2nd July 2011 till date

The Presbyterian Education System stands as follows:
- The Proprietor of the schools is the Presbyterian Church in Cameroon represented by the Moderator, the Rt. Rev. Fonki Samuel Forba.
- The Presbyterian Education Secretary Mr. Njie Samuel Kale, is the administrative head.
- The Managers of Schools

Mission Statement

The Mission of the Presbyterian Church in Cameroon is to proclaim the good news of God, through Jesus Christ, in word and action. The proclamation of this good news includes THE PREACHING OF THE WORD, TEACHING, HEALING AND LIBERATING THE PEOPLE OF GOD FROM SIN (Luke 4:18-19).

In this wise the Presbyterian Education Authority (PEA) shall strive to:

a). Provide devoted, sustainable and affordable high moral, quality Education to all, at all times within available resources.
b). Provide such Education wherever and whenever possible and under appropriate conditions in a supplementary and complementary rather than competitive manner, and in compliance with all status governing Education in Cameroon.
c). Provide particularly Education, which is society based.
d). Provide Education to the young people of the urban and the rural areas of Cameroon.
e). Fulfill this Mission with a deep commitment to human dignity and basic human rights, and the moral and ethical obligations of the Education profession.

The Presbyterian Education Authority (PEA) is out to proclaim the Good News of God through Jesus Christ in the TEACHING MINISTRY, of the Presbyterian Church in Cameroon. The Presbyterian Church in Cameroon is the historical and constitutional successor of the BASEL MISSION CHURCH IN KAMERUN, established in 1886 as an external arm of the Evangelical Missionary Society of BASEL (BASEL MISSION) in Switzerland. It maintains the spiritual and theological continuity of that Church, and upholds the Reformed Tradition.

The Basel Mission (BM)

The Basel Mission is an Evangelical Missionary Society founded in Basel, Switzerland, in 1815. Its main objective was the propagation of the Gospel of Jesus Christ to the uttermost parts of the world. The Mission Society was already at work in India, Indonesia, North Borneo, Hong Kong, Ghana and Nigeria before Kamerun in 1886. In every station, mission stations and schools were built. When the Germans annexed Cameroon in

1884, the English Baptists who had established in the Coastal towns and villages of Cameroon found it very difficult to work under them.

The Basel Mission was persuaded to take over the work of the English Baptist Missionaries. This was reluctantly accepted and the first Basel Mission Missionaries arrived in Cameroon on the 23rd December 1886. These were Gottlieb Munz, Yohannes Bitzer, Christian Dilger and Frederick Becher.

The Mission Stations that were taken over from the English Baptist Missionaries included Bimbia, Douala and Ambas Bay. Between 1886 and 1897, Basel Mission Stations were established at Bonaberi in 1889, Buea in 1891, Lobetal in 1892, Nyasoso in 1896, Edea and Bombe in the year 1897.

Between 1900 and 1914, stations were established in Bali in 1903, Foumban in 1906, Bagham in 1909, Bangwa in 1911, Besongabang, Ndogbea, Bandzun and Bana in 1913, Babungo in 1914, when the First World War broke out.

REFERENCES

A. Books
Atogho T.T., *Basel Mission Schools become Presbyterian Schools*, Victoria, 1966.
Autenrieth F., *Chez les Balis*, Translated from German in 1905 by Krieg E., Geneva, 1905.
Berman E.H., (ed.), *African Reactions to Missionary Education*, New York, Teachers College Press, 1975.
Chilver E.M., *Zintgraff's Explorations in Bamenda, Adamawa and the Benue lands, 1889-1892*, Buea, Government Press, 1966.
Coleman J.S., *Nigeria, Background to Nationalism*, Los Angeles, University of California Press, 1971.
Graham C.K., *The history of Education in Ghana: from the Earliest Times to the Declaration of Independence*, London, Frank Cass, 1971.
Guifford, P., and Louis, W.R., (eds.), *Britain and Germany in Africa - Imperial Rivalry and Colonial Rule*, New Haven, Yale University Press, 1967.
Hallden, E. *The Culture Policy of the Basel Mission in the Cameroons, 1886-1905,* Lund, University of Upsala Press; 1968.
Hausz K., *Aus dem Leben von F. Ernst der Pionier der Bali Mission*, Basel, 1912.
Keller W., *The History of the Presbyterian Church in West Cameroon*, Victoria, Presbook., 1969.
Lekunze E.F., *A Historical and Comparative Analysis of the Evangelistic Strategy of the Basel Mission*, Ph.D., Chicago, 1987.
Madiba E., *Colonisation et Evangelisation en Afrique:*
L'heritage scholaire au Cameroon (1885-1956), Bern, Editions Peter Lang., 1980.
Mbuagbaw T.F., and Brian R., *The History of Cameroon*, London, Longmans, 1987.
Raflaub F., *Gebt uns Lehrer, Gegenwartsaufgabe der Basler Mission in Kamerun*, Basel, 1948.
Rudin H., *Germans in the Cameroons, 1884-1914: a Case Study in*

Modern Imperialism, New Haven, 1938.
Rubin N., *Cameroon: An African Federation*, London, Pall Mall, 1971.
Shu, S.N., *Landmarks in Cameroon Education*, Limbe, NOOREMAC Press, 1985.
Stoecker, H. (Ed). *German Imperialism in Africa: from the beginning until the Second World War*. Translated by Bernd Zolner. New Jersey: Hurst and Company, 1986. Van-Slageren J., *Les Origines de l'Eglise Evangelique du Cameroun*, Leiden, E. J. Brill., 1972.
Warneck G., *Outline of a History of Protestant Missions*, Edinburgh, 1901.

B. Articles

Basel Mission Cameroon, "Une Exploration à Bali" in *Le Missionaire*, No. 1, January 1903.
Ekiti E. A. " Education: The Fight against Ignorance," in Nyansako-ni-Nku, (ed.), *Journey In Faith: The Story of the Presbyterian Church in Cameroon* Buma Kor &
Co Publishers, 1982.
Fohtung, M. G., "Self-Portrait of a Cameroonian", in *Paideuma*, No. 38, 1992.
Gensichen, H. W., "Evangelisation and Civilisation: The Germans", in *International Bulletin of Missionary Research*, No. 6, 1982.
Gôhring M., "Mitteilungen aus den neuesten Berichten, Kamerun, Grasland" in *Der evanglische Heidenbote*, 1910.
Kala Lobe, "Douala Manga Bell, Heros de la Resistance Douala" in *Grandes Figures Africaines de la Xxe siecle*, Tournai, 1977.
"Memorandum on Educational Policy in Nigeria" in *Sessional Paper*, No.20, 1947.
Schuler, "Im lande der Bali," in *Evangelissche Missions Magazin of 1903*.

Reports

Report to the Trusteeship Council of the United Nations, the 1949 Education Ordinance.
Report to the United Nations Trusteeship Council, 1949. Report to the United Nations Trusteeship Council for 1956
indicating the opening of the Queen of Holy Rosary Secondary School, Okoyong.
Report to the U.N.O. 1949.
Report to the U.N. O., 1953.
Report to the U.N.O. for 1954.

Report to the U.N.O. for 1955.
Report to the U.N.O. to 1956.
Theses and Dissertations
Booth B.F., "A Comparative Study of Mission and Government Involvement in Educational Development in West Cameroon, 1922-1969", Ph.D., UCLA, 1973.
Dah J. N., Missionary Motivations and Methods: A Critical Examination of the Basel Mission in Cameroon 1886 1914, Ph.D., Basel, 1983.
Goodridge R., "Society and Economy in British Cameroon 1916-61", Ph.D., Ibadan, 1988.
Gwanfogbe M.B, "Changing Regimes and the Development of Education in Cameroon" Ph D. London, 1995.
Lekunze E.F., "Chieftaincy and Christianity in Cameroon, 1886-1926: A Historical and Evangelical Strategy of the Basel Mission", Ph.D., Chicago, 1987.
Raaflaub F., "Gebt uns Lehrer, Geschchte und Gegenwartsaufgabe der Basler Mission Kamerun", Ph D. Basel, 1948.
Shu S.N., "The collaboration policy in Cameroon Education, 1910-1931: a Study of the Policy of collaboration between Government and Voluntary Agencies", Ph D., London, 1972.

E. Archival Materials

a. *Basel Mission Archives (BASEL MISSIONA)*

BASEL MISSIONA. E-1., Preliminary discussions about Cameroon Mission containing correspondence between the Basel Mission and Baptist Missionary Society as well as with the German Government.
BASEL MISSIONA. E-2., Letters and Reports on Members of the Mission since Arrival in Cameroon.
BASEL MISSIONA.E-2.3., Kamerun 1890, Basel Mission's relations with the Baptist Christians.
BASEL MISSIONA.E-2.3., Kamerun 1890, Joseph Wilson, a Cameroonian Baptist Pastor appealing for a separation of the Baptists from the Basel Mission.
BASEL MISSIONA. E-2.2., Kamerun 1889, the Basel Mission's Request to Divide the Territory between the Denominations.
BASEL MISSIONA.E-2.4., Kamerun 1891, Report on Bethel School.
BASEL MISSIONA.E-2.9., Kamerun 1896, Reports made in 1896 on the conflicts between Basel Missionaries in
Cameroon.
BASEL MISSIONA.E-2.11., Kamerun 1898, Report by Schuler, the

Inspector of Schools.
BASEL MISSIONA.E-2.8., Kamerun 1895, Letters and Reports from Lobethal Station
BASEL MISSIONA.E-2.11., Kamerun 1898, Letters and Reports from the Station at Mangamba.
BASEL MISSIONA.E-2.12., Kamerun 1899, Letters and Reports from Edea Station.
BASEL MISSIONA.E-2.15., Kamerun 1902, Letters and Reports from Nyasoso Station.
BASEL MISSIONA.E-2.15., Kamerun 1902, Entrance Selection into Bonaberi School.
BASEL MISSIONA.E-2.10., Kamerun 1897, Draft Curriculum for use in Mission Secondary Schools.
BASEL MISSIONA.E-2.16., Kamerun 1903, Report by Stutz and Deibol on the German School in Bonanjo.
BASEL MISSIONA.E-2.10., Kamerun 1897, Curriculum in Mission Secondary Schools.
BASEL MISSIONA.E-2.10., Kamerun 1897, Minutes of the General Conference of Missionaries.
BASEL MISSIONA.E-2.10., Kamerun 1897, Basel Mission School Curriculum.
BASEL MISSIONA.E-2.16., Kamerun 1903, The new Station at Bali.
BASEL MISSIONA.E-2.13., Kamerun 1900, Minutes of a Conference on Schools.
BASEL MISSIONA.E-2.16., Kamerun 1903, Minutes of Annual Conference of Teachers.
BASEL MISSIONA.E-2.16., Kamerun 1903, Minutes of Mission Teachers Annual Conference.
BASEL MISSIONA.E-2.31., Kamerun 1910, vol.1 Dinkelacker, Inspector of Basel Mission Schools and Lutz, Field Board Chairman, Report on new Government School Regulations.
BASEL MISSIONA.E-2.34., Kamerun 1911 vol. 11, Minute of a Teachers' Conference.
BASEL MISSIONA.E-2.11., Kamerun 1898, Schuler's Report on Schools.
BASEL MISSIONA.E-2.11., Kamerun, 1898, Report on the Middle School and Seminary at Bonaberi.
BASEL MISSIONA.E-2.23., Kamerun 1907 vol. 1, Dinkerlacker's Report on Buea Middle School.
BASEL MISSIONA.E-2.21., Kamerun 1906, Inspector's Report on Schools.

BASEL MISSIONA.E-2.35., Kamerun 1912 vol.1, Report of General Conference at Douala, April 1912.
BASEL MISSIONA.E-1., Preliminary Discussions about the Cameroon Mission
BASEL MISSIONA.E-2.11., Kamerun 1898, Petition by Inspector Oehler of the Basel Mission to the Colonial Office against Expropriation of land.
BASEL MISSIONA.E-2.15., Kamerun, 1902, Government Policy on the Distribution of Crown Land.
BASEL MISSIONA.E-2.16., Kamerun 1903, Lutz and the Land Commission in Respect to Buea Area.
BASEL MISSIONA.E-2.19., Kamerun 1905, Labour in the German Plantations.
BASEL MISSIONA.E-2.11., Kamerun 1898, Gohring's Petition against the Sale of Liquor.
BASEL MISSIONA.E-16., Kamerun 1903, Letters and Reports from Bali station.
BASEL MISSIONA.E-2.22., Kamerun 1906, vol.11, Letters and Reports from Bamum Station.
BASEL MISSIONA.E.2.32., Kamerun 1910 vol.11, Report Written by Gohring on Chief Njoya's School in Bamum.
BASEL MISSIONA.E-2.33., Kamerun 1911 vol.1, Vohringer's Application to Baptise a Polygamist.
BASEL MISSIONA.E-2.15., Kamerun 1902, Preparation for Mission Work in Bali.
BASEL MISSIONA.E-2.15., Kamerun 1902, Report on Possible Takeover of the American Presbyterian Mission Stations.
BASEL MISSIONA.E-4.4, 1914-1924, Letters from Cameroon.
BASEL MISSIONA.E-4.7., Correspondence with ex-Basel Missionaries in the service of the Paris Evangelical Mission in Cameroon.
BASEL MISSIONA.E-5.2., 1940, Report of the Basel Mission Board meeting,
BASEL MISSIONA.E-5.2., 1944, Report of the Inspector of schools to the Home Board.
BASEL MISSIONA.E-5.3., Annual reports by Field Missionaries, 1925-1948.
BASEL MISSIONA.E-5.2., Annual Report by Field Missionaries, 1934.
BASEL MISSIONA.E-5.7., Correspondence Concerning School Work, 1927-1933.
BASEL MISSIONA.E-5.7., Correspondence between Field Missionaries and the Home Board, (1927-1933).

b. National Archives Buea (NAB)
NAB. Ba. 192 1., Annual Report by Ruxton. NAB.Ba 1921-1923., Reports from Mamfe.
NAB. Ba. 1925., Report to the League of Nations.
NAB.Ba. 1927., Correspondence between Government and Teachers.
NAB.Ba.1927., Report to the League of Nations.
NAB.Ba.1926., Annual Report; Return of German Planters and Missionaries.
NAB. Ba 1924/1., Annual Report for 1924.
NAB. Ab/a 1932/7., Cameroon Memorandum of Evidence before the Elliot Commission, 1943.
NAB.Ba,1927., Report to the League of Nations.

IMC LONDON
IMC/CBASEL MISSIONS Box 276., Correspondence between J.H. Oldham and Oettli of the Basel Mission Home Board.
IMC/CBASEL MISSIONS. Box 276., problems of the Basel Mission adjusting to the British System.
IMC/CBASEL MISSIONS, Box 276., Correspondence between S.M. Grier, Director of Education and J.H. Oldham of IMC., in respect of a Memorandum on difficulties regarding "Bush schools" in Cameroon by W. Oettli of the Basel Mission, 1927-1929.
IMC/CBASEL MISSIONS Box 276, Meeting on the registration of village school teachers, 1927.
IMC/CBASEL MISSIONS Box 276., Correspondence between the Colonial Office, British Missionary societies, International Council of Protestant Missions and the German Missions from 1916 to1924.

PCA (PRESBYTERIAN CHURCH ARCHIVE)
S. 505/2093 of June 1963, Correspondence by the Education Secretary to Basel.
PCA. Arrey-Mbi S.B. "A Look at the College Log Book", 1974 unpublished.
PCA. S. Lec/9089 of 22nd June, 1955 by Basel Mission Supervisor of Schools.
PCA. 1964., Information from the Presbyterian Education Secretary's Office.
PCA., The first Youth Pastor: Rev. Miaz.
PCA. 1961, Principal's report on admission.
PCA. Principals report suBasel Missionitted to the Board of Governors

on 16 May 1964.
PCA. S. vii/5/3613, Gopfert H., Supervisor of Basel Mission schools Annual Report, 16 April, 1953.
PCA., Principals Annual Report for 1959 SuBasel Missionitted to the Board of Governors.
PCA., Principals Annual Report for 1960 SuBasel Missionitted
to the Board of Governors on 4 November 1960. PCA. 1952., Annual Report by the Supervisor of Schools. PCA. S. Lec/9089 of 22nd June 1955 by Supervisor of Basel
Mission Schools.

INDEX

Abandeng, Monica. *See* Makaya episode
Adamawa 29, 123
Allegret, Rev. 65
American Presbyterian Missionary Society 28
Aufklärung 11. *See also* enlightenment

Bachman, Rev. Willy 113
Bagam 50
Bakundu-Banga 17
Bakweri 44, 45, 102
Bakweri Development Union 102
Bali
  Bali people 46
  Cameroon Protestant College Bali 90
  CPC Bali x, 89
  Fon Fonyonga x, 35, 54, 55, 57
  Galega I 54, 59
  Lima of Bali 56, 66
  Mungaka, language of Bali 19, 20, 21, 24, 47, 69, 70, 80
  Zintgraff 54
Balitruppe 46
Bamenda xv, 54, 66, 86, 92, 102, 109, 123
  Bamenda Improvement Association 102
  Grassfields 19, 20, 21, 33, 47, 54, 55, 110, 112
  Mankon 86, 87, 94, 113
Bamileke country 66
Bamum 48, 50, 56, 57, 60, 61, 127
  Banjoun 50
Bana 50, 121

Bangwa 50, 121
Banso 94
baptism 18, 57, 60, 62
Baptist Missionary Society vii, 9, 13, 14, 15, 17, 26, 28, 30, 37, 43, 50, 125
Basel Missionaries
  Rittman 15
Basel Missionary Society xvi, 1, 2, 3
Basel Mission College x, xvi, 88, 90, 91
Basel Mission House Bali x, 55
Basel Mission in Mamfe 67
Basel Mission Trading Company 47
Basler Evangelische Missionsgesellschaft 1
Basler Missionshandlungsgesellschaft 47
Batanga 28
Becher, Rev. Friederich 17, 121
Bell, King 54
Bell, Rudolf Douala Manga 20
Berlin Conference, the 15
Besongabang x, 50, 69, 73, 74, 91, 121
Bethel 17, 20, 125
Binetsch, Rev. 15
Bizer, Rev. Johannes 17, 23
Bohner, Heinrich vii, 26, 32
Bombe 23, 50, 69, 121
Bonabela 24
Bonaberi 23, 38, 40, 50, 121, 126
Bonaku 25, 50
Bonanjo 24, 126
Bonner 15
boys' school. *See* Bali Mittelschule 22, 23, 34

| 131

Bremen 12, 14
Bremen conference 12
British Baptist Mission 15, 18
British Baptist Missionaries 16, 17, 30
British Baptist Missionary Society vii, 9, 13, 14, 17, 26, 30, 43
British Baptists in Victoria 47
British Southern Cameroons 1, 68, 78, 101
Buea ii, x, xv, 8, 22, 23, 38, 40, 45, 50, 69, 70, 73, 84, 100, 113, 121, 123, 126, 127, 128
  girls' schools 84
  Government Teachers Training College 73
  handing over ceremony 113
  Sasse 87, 100, 102, 103
Bulu 28
Bush schools 66, 128

Cameroon Baptist Convention 90
Cameroon Development Corporation xvi, 93, 102
Cameroon Development Corporation Workers' Union 102
Cameroon Protestant College Bali 90
Cameroon's Union College 90
Cameroon Welfare Union xvi, 100, 102
Chilver, E. xv, 54, 60, 123
Christaller, Theodore 26, 34, 54
Colonial Welfare and Development Fund 78
Conference of Protestant Missionary Society 61
Congo 14, 28
Congregation du St. Esprit et du St. Coeur de Marie 29
CPC x, xvi, 89, 90, 91
  O'Neil 87
cultural relativism 61

Dah, Jonas 6, 61, 125

Debrunner, H.W. 3, 115
Dehon, Mgr. 29
Denton, Captain 100
Deutsche Gesellschaaft zur Beforderung reiner Lehre und Wahrer Gottseligkeit 10
Dibonge, R.J.K. 101
Dibundi, Joshua 18, 30, 31
Dilger, Rev. Christian 17, 121
Dinkelacker 36, 39, 40, 62, 126
Din, Modi 69
Din, Ngosso 20
Diso, Rev. Peter Essoka 109
Dobell, General 64
Donat, R. 31
Douala 15, 17, 19, 20, 21, 24, 26, 31, 33, 38, 40, 45, 46, 47, 48, 50, 54, 58, 65, 66, 69, 80, 121, 124, 127
Drang nach Schulbildung 71
Dr. Good 28
Dr. Johnston 28

Ebai, J.T. 112
Edea 23, 50, 121, 126
Eglise Evangélique de Paris 2
Eglise Evangélique du Cameroun 2, 6
Ekeze, Pastor Johannes Litumbe 66, 69
Ekiti, Eugene xi, 6, 110, 111, 119, 124
Elat 28
Elementary Teachers Training Centre 81
Elliot's Commission 102
Endeley, E.M.L. 102
enlightenment 11
enlightenment, age of 11
Equatorial Guinea 66
Ernst, F. 55, 59, 123
Eseh, Samuel Mbong 91
Ethiopia 67
Ethiopianism 67
Evangelical Mission of Basel 10

Fabri, Friedrich 12
Female Education viii, 84
First World War 2, 5, 19, 30, 45, 50, 51, 52, 62, 63, 64, 79, 96, 121
Foncha, J.N. 95
Fonta 92
forest regions 104
Foumban 50, 57, 121
Fusi, Mfobe 84

Galega 54, 55, 59
Galega I, Fon 54, 59
Gehilfenschule 25
German Baptist Mission 30, 31, 51
German Baptist Missionary 30, 31
German colonial culture 9
German Pallotine Mission 29
German Schools 24, 40
German Schools (Deutsche Schulen) 24
German society for the furtherance of pure learning and true spirituality 10
German South West Africa 12
Göhring 60
Gold Coast 3, 9, 12, 15, 16, 17, 20, 67, 73, 94
Grest, J. 73, 83

Hallden, Erik 10, 12, 61, 123
Hamburg 13
Hedge schools 66
Heiser 73
Helpers' School (Gehilfenschule) 25
Higher Elementary Teachers' Training College 103
Hope Wadel secondary school 87
Hummel 73

India 9, 16, 20, 67, 120
Inter-Denominational Missionary Conference 68
International Conference of Mission Societies xvi, 67
International Council of Protestant Missions xvi, 3, 68, 128
Islam 48, 57, 60

Joseph Merrick College 91
Jua, A. N. 95
Junior Cambridge Examination 73

Kamerun Ex-servicemen National Union xvi, 102
Keller, Werner 5, 15, 109, 113, 123
Knabenschule 22
Kribi 28
Kumba 85, 86, 91, 92, 103, 109, 112
  Girls' Teacher Training College 85
  Rural Training Centres 92
  Saint Francis Teachers' Training College 85

Labour Exploitation 45
Lafon, Hon. 95
Lake Mohonk Conference of the International Council of Missions 67
Language Policy 46
League of Nations 2, 3, 99, 128
Legislative Council of Nigeria 102
Lennartz, F.J. 29
Lima, Francis 56, 66
Lobatel 23
Lobatel Middle school 23
Lolodorf 28
London Baptist Missionary 50, 99
Lyonga, Catherine 84

Macauley, Herbert 100
Madiba, E. 6, 123

Makaya, episode 67
Mamfe 67, 86, 92, 100, 102, 109, 128
Mamfe Improvement Association 102
Mancho, J.F. 110, 112
Mangamba 23, 40, 50, 126
Middle School 22, 23, 38, 39, 40, 87, 126
Middle Schools 22, 23, 24, 34, 37, 38, 39, 40, 50, 74
Mill Hill Fathers 64, 65
Mill Hill Missionary Society 3
Mill Hill Mission, Catholic 86
Mission 21 xv, 4, 7
Mofor, ATM 91
Muna, Solomon Tandeng x, 83, 94
Mungaka 19, 20, 21, 24, 47, 69, 70, 80. *See also* Bali
Mungo 17
Munz, George 37
Munz, Rev. Gottlieb 17, 19, 37, 121

Nachtigal 53
Namibia 12. *See also* German South West Africa
national archives, Buea 8
Native Administration Infant Schools 99
Native Baptist Church 18, 30, 31
Ndamukong, Hon. 94
Ndi, Anthony 63
Ndogbea 50, 121
Ndongue 50
Ndu 91
Ngole, Rt. Rev Abraham xi, 84, 93, 112
Ngoo, S.M. 102
Nigeria 8, 73, 81, 85, 87, 94, 99, 102, 103, 120, 123, 124
  Calabar 87
  Enugu 70
  Ibadan xv, 8, 125
  Lagos 70, 72
Nigerian Education Code 70
Nigerian National Democratic Party xvi, 100
Njinikom 29, 94
Njoya 56, 57, 60, 127
Njoya, King 56, 57, 60, 127. *See also* Bamum
Nkwe, George 18, 30
Normal School 73
North German Missionary Society 15
Ntoko, R.M. 112
Nyasaland 67
Nyasoso x, 23, 40, 50, 69, 73, 81, 82, 87, 91, 114, 121, 126

Oehler, Theodor 14, 19, 25, 127
Oldham, John 2, 68, 128
O'Neil, D. H. 87
Ozimba, J.A. x, 88

Palloti, Cardinal 29
Pallotine Fathers 19, 65. *See also* Pallotine Missions
Pallotine Mission 29
PCC archives, the 8
Peyer, Rev. E. 109
Phelps-Stokes, Caroline 68
Phelps-Stokes Commission 68
Post-WW1 Missionary Resumption vii, 2
Preliminary Teacher Training Centre 81
Presbyterian Church in Cameroon xv, xvi, 1, 6, 86, 93, 108, 119, 120, 124
Presbyterian Church in Southern Cameroons 1, 86
Presbyterian Church in West Cameroon xvi, 1, 3, 5, 123
Public Records Office, London xv, xvi, 8

Queen of the Holy Rosary Secondary

School 86
Queen, Victoria 53

Raaflaub, Fritz x, 7, 62, 77, 125
Religious Instruction 20, 38
Rival Missionary Societies vii, 28
Roman Catholic Mission 18, 19, 26, 28, 44, 64, 85, 102
Roman Catholic Missionary Society. See Mill Hill
Rudin, Dr. Peter x, 28, 30, 62, 78, 89, 90, 123
Rudin, Harry x, 28, 30, 62, 78, 89, 90, 123
Rural Training Centres xvi, 92
Rutherford 100

Sacerdotes Cordis Jesu xvi, 29
Sacred Heart Fathers 28
Sacred Heart Mission 29
Saint Francis Teachers' Training College 85
Sakbayeme 23, 40, 50
Saker Baptist College 91
Sanaga, River 23
Schneider, J.P. 73, 88
Schuler, Rev. 35
Schultz, Miss 91
Secondary Education viii, 87
Second World War 64, 78, 79, 84, 93, 100, 107, 109, 124
Shisong 29
Shu, Rev. Jacob 109, 111
Shu, S.N. 5
Shu, Solomon 63
Silver Jubilee, PCC 6
SOAS, London xvi, 3, 8
Societé des Missions Évangeliques de Paris 64, 65
Sosiga, Tita 56
Steffens, August 31
Su, Rev. Aaron 113

Switzerland 8, 10, 16, 36, 109, 120
Basel Mission house in 8
Sydney Philipson's Report, Sir 81

Technical Education viii, 91
Tiko 66, 69, 92
Togo 12
Traditional rulers 67
Tubingen 10

Ulmann 73
United Nations Organization 2
United Nations Trusteeship Council 80, 124
University of London xv, 3, 8

Van-Slageren, Jean 6, 124
Venn, Henry 25
Vernacular or Village / Bush Schools 21
Vernacular schools 69, 99. See also village schools
Vernacular Schools xi, 17, 46, 47, 72, 79, 80, 93, 96
Victoria 5, 15, 17, 22, 26, 47, 50, 53, 69, 76, 79, 84, 85, 91, 92, 100, 109, 123
  Saker Baptist College 91
Victoria, Queen 15
Vieter, Father Heinrich 18, 29
Vohringer, Pastor 62, 127
Von Bismarck, Otto 13, 29
Von Puttkamer, Governor Jesco x, 57, 58
Von Soden, Julius x, 13

Walters, Cable ii, 91
Warneck, Gustav 11, 12, 61, 124
Weber, Lina x, 31, 84, 85, 86
  Na Weber. See German South West Africa

Weik, Rev. Father 29
West African German Commercial
    Syndicate 16
Whitt, Donald x, 89
Williams, J.M. 102
Woerman, Company 13
Woermann, Adolf 13, 16
Women's Teacher Training College xvi,
    86
Württemburg 11, 34
Wurttemburg, Germans of 10

Yaoundé 8, 28

Zintgraff, Eugen 54, 59, 123

www.ingramcontent.com/pod-product-compliance
Lightning Source LLC
Chambersburg PA
CBHW070737230426
43669CB00014B/2486